The Cambridge Manuals of Science and
Literature

T0352301

COPARTNERSHIP IN INDUSTRY

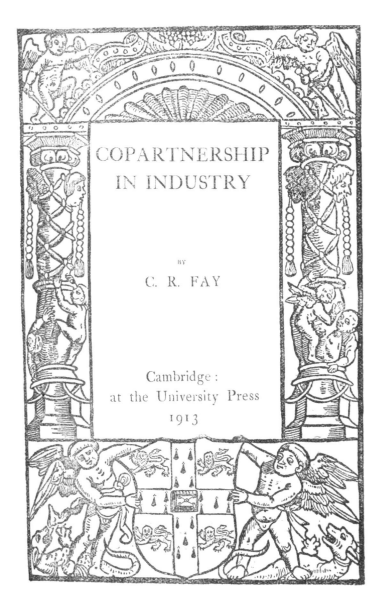

COPARTNERSHIP
IN INDUSTRY

BY

C. R. FAY

Cambridge:
at the University Press

1913

CAMBRIDGE UNIVERSITY PRESS
Cambridge, New York, Melbourne, Madrid, Cape Town,
Singapore, São Paulo, Delhi, Tokyo, Mexico City

Cambridge University Press
The Edinburgh Building, Cambridge CB2 8RU, UK

Published in the United States of America by Cambridge University Press, New York

www.cambridge.org
Information on this title: www.cambridge.org/9781107692701

First published 1913
First paperback edition 2011

A catalogue record for this publication is available from the British Library

ISBN 978-1-107-69270-1 Paperback

*With the exception of the coat of arms at
the foot, the design on the title page is a
reproduction of one used by the earliest known
Cambridge printer, John Siberch,* 1521

CONTENTS

COPARTNERSHIP IN
INDUSTRY

CHAPTER I

THE HISTORY AND SPIRIT OF COPARTNERSHIP

" WHEN a business is thriving, a certain surplus is earned above the ordinary rate of profit and wages in that business. . . . It is this perpetually recurring struggle for a surplus which is itself only occasional and precarious, and not determinable beforehand by fixed laws, or even reasonable anticipation, which is the fundamental reason of the existence and powers of trades unions." [1] So wrote Herman Merivale, sometime Professor of Political Economy at Oxford in an Appendix to the Report of the Royal Commission on Trades Unions in 1868. His colleagues in the Majority Report remarked that " the habitual code of sentiment which prevailed between employers and workmen in the times when the former were regarded by both law and usage as the governing class is now greatly relaxed, and cannot be revived. A

[1] 11th and Final Report, p. 122.

substitute has now to be found for it, arising from the feelings of equity and enlightened self-interest and mutual forbearance, which should exist between contracting parties who can best promote their several chances of advantage by aiding and accommodating each other." [1]

The immediate object of the Commission was the provision of a more suitable legal status for the Trade Union, but they nevertheless devoted some attention to two methods for the avoidance of industrial strife, which seemed to deserve commendation.

One of these was the method of arbitration and conciliation. A. T. Mundella, a Nottingham manufacturer, explained to them the good work which he had accomplished with his Board of Conciliation in the glove and hosiery trade. Rupert Kettle, a County Court Judge of Worcestershire, testified to similar success in the building trades of the Midlands. The voluntary Boards of Arbitration and Conciliation, thus instituted in the 'sixties, have since been extended to other trades, notably to iron and steel and to coal-mining. Their voluntary character has been preserved throughout. But neither the voluntary system of England, nor the compulsory system of New Zealand, nor the intermediate system of Canada, has been able to eliminate industrial warfare. At the best, arbitration and

[1] 11th and Final Report, p. 17.

conciliation do but assist to preserve an armed and precarious peace.

The second device of which the Commissioners of 1868 took some account was the scheme of profit-sharing which was at that time in successful opera-tion at the Yorkshire collieries of Henry Briggs, Son and Co., Ltd. The scheme lasted from 1865 to 1874 and, to quote Mr Sedley Taylor,[1] " the strong language of approval held concerning the experiment while its success was still unimpaired, in the writings of Mill, Fawcett, and Thornton, gave to it a still wider notoriety and caused the most sanguine expectations to be founded on the continued prosperity augured for the system. When the abandonment of profit-sharing at the Whitwood Collieries became publicly known, the feeling of disappointment and discouragement was there-fore proportionately widespread." In 1865 Henry Briggs & Son, hitherto a private company, registered themselves under the Act of 1862 as a joint stock company with limited liability. Two thirds of the capital was retained by the partners and the other third was offered to the public, preference being given to applications for shares from officials and operatives employed in the business and from customers purchasing the produce of the collieries. The most novel feature was introduced by the

[1] " Profit-Sharing," p. 133.

following clause in the prospectus :—" In order, however, to associate capital and labour still more intimately, the founders of the company will recommend to the shareholders that whenever the divisible profits accruing from the business shall (after the usual reservation for redemption of capital and other legitimate allowances) exceed 10 per cent. on the capital embarked, all those employed by the company, whether as managers or agents at fixed salaries, or as workpeople, shall receive one half of such excess profit as a bonus, to be distributed amongst them in proportion to, and as a percentage upon, their respective earnings during the year in which such profit shall have accrued."

These proposals were in the direction of what is to-day called industrial copartnership. The originators looked for two advantages from their adoption, the cessation of labour troubles and an increase in the economies of working ; and by 1868 they were of the opinion that both these objects had been attained. Whereas during the ten years from 1853 there had been acute tension and intermittent strikes, since 1865 there had been scarcely a single play day and the working of the collieries had been infinitely smoother. No opposition was offered to the men joining the Union, and, though the Methley district was declared to be a hotbed of Unionism, yet only 5 per

cent. were in fact members. " I do not think,"
said Mr H. C. Briggs, "that our men would think
of appealing to the Union now." [1]   Furthermore,
the economies in timber and stores had been great.
" When the men pass through the yards, they pick
up bolts or nails, saying, ' This is so much bonus
saved.' Previously, I have known of men, where
they had to put in a piece of rail, breaking a new
rail in two in order to get the proper length, and
then bury it in the dirt if they broke it the wrong
length, and break another. Now you never hear
of anything of that kind happening." [2]   In 1872,
however, the old labour trouble reappeared. In
that year the Miners' Union decided to hold a
demonstration on the day fixed for the general
meeting of shareholders at which the bonus would
be voted. The men were practically forced to
choose between Unionism and Copartnership.
About one-third attended the demonstration, and
forfeited their bonus for the current year as well
as all claim to future bonus. In 1874 a dispute
arose about the use of riddles for sifting coal in the
pits, and the men supported the Union against
the Company. In 1875 they struck work in con-
junction with the employees of other collieries as
a protest against a reduction in the district rate of

[1] Royal Commission on Trades Unions, Q. 12,623.
[2] *Ibid*, Q. 12,714.

wages, and the next shareholders' meeting voted the abolition of profit-sharing.

The Trade Unions opposed the Briggs' scheme because they considered it likely to weaken if not to destroy their power. The evidence just quoted from Mr H. C. Briggs shows that this fear was well-founded. But there were also certain features in the scheme itself which contributed to its breakdown. In the first place, the agreement between the Company and the men was loosely framed. The shareholders might, without previous notice, decline to vote the bonus for the past year, and they might if they so pleased, grant it to some workers while refusing it to others. In the second place, the management declared it to be in keeping with the intention of the agreement that the initial interest paid on the shareholders' capital should vary with the fluctuations of current wages. These two things gave to the scheme an air of uncertainty and inconsistency, and the course of events brought the latter failing into vivid relief. For whereas in 1873, after a year of exceptional prosperity the initial interest on capital was raised from 10 to 15 per cent., in the following year, 1874, when the conditions of the trade necessitated a reduction in wages,[1] no proposal was made to reduce pro-

[1] For the violent fall in coal-miners' wages after 1873, see Bowley, "Wages in the Nineteenth Century," pp. 105 and 131.

portionately the shareholders' dividend. In the third place, the plan of inducing employees to take shares in the Company by giving employee shareholders a higher rate of bonus was badly conceived. From the evidence given to the Commission in 1868[1] it is clear that there was disagreement between the managers and certain of the workers on this point. The managers inclined to an equal rate for all on the ground that, one worker having as good a claim as another, discrimination would lead to complications. The most ardent advocates from among the workers, however, argued for a higher rate to employee shareholders and pleaded that such share-holding, in addition to improving permanently the social status of the men, gave breadth and stability to the scheme of profit-sharing. Indeed, they blamed the management for the fact that by 1868, when over £7000 had been distributed in bonus, only 150 shares of £10 each were held by workers. But though the policy adopted by the managers may have incidentally contributed to this result, yet they certainly did not intend it.[2] For they were prepared to associate the employees, not only in shareholding, but also in direction. In 1869, at the instance of Mr Archibald Briggs, a working shareholder was elected by his fellow-workers as one of the five directors of the Company.

[1] *Cf.* Qs. 12,637 ; 13,022.   [2] *Cf.* Q. 12,754.

It is perhaps misleading to begin a record of Copartnership with a great failure ; for since then there have been some great and enduring successes. But the Briggs' scheme was the first great experiment in industrial copartnership by British employers : and the date of its occurrence, 1865 to 1874, is highly significant. It came between the Limited Liability Act of 1862 and the last of the Acts enfranchising Trade Unions in 1875. Limited liability has made possible a vast extension of that most remarkable form of modern industrial structure, the public joint stock company. All through the nineteenth century the growth in the size of businesses has been making the relation between employer and employee less personal. The public company accentuates this impersonality. The managers and foremen alone come into constant contact with the company's employees, and the general policy of the company is determined by a board of directors acting on behalf of distant and scattered shareholders. This division of responsibility is sometimes a source of financial weakness, and is certainly a moral danger. The shareholders surrender their conscience to the directors, and the directors excuse their actions on the plea of protecting their shareholders' interests. "We felt also that we were responsible to a large body of outside shareholders, many of whom had placed in our hands the hardly-earned savings of years, confiding in our capacity and discretion ; and the great majority of whom cared little for our experiment except in so far as it might increase or diminish their own dividends." [1] In this familiar strain Mr Archibald Briggs subsequently justified the action of his company in raising the shareholders' initial dividend.

The public company communicates with the shareholders, the owners of its property, by balance sheets : and the publication of profits is a great advantage when some of these are to be shared with the workers. But this advantage is largely offset by the complexities of capitalisation. The usual way of stating the financial case for Co-partnership is that capital ought to get a moderate initial remuneration, say 5 per cent., which corresponds to the wages of labour, and that further profit beyond this should be shared between the two. But 5 per cent. on watered capital may be a highly immoderate return, and 5 per cent. on original improved capital a very low return. Moreover, it frequently happens that the issue of new capital is associated with a preference to existing shareholders who receive in effect a present of profit. If the business is one which practises profit-sharing, the shareholders then get a present out of profits in which the workers do not share, unless

[1] Sedley Taylor, "Profit-Sharing," p. 152.

the contingency has been provided for in advance. The obscurity of profits which is one of the obstacles to Copartnership when the firm is in private hands is not really removed when the firm is a public company. One criticism made against Briggs & Co., was that in 1873 when a sum of £30,000 was taken out of the previous year's profits and invested in a mine the shareholders got new shares in respect of it, but the employees lost the £15,000 of bonus which would otherwise have come to them as their share in the divisible profit. The organisation, therefore, of the public company, while it increases the impersonality of the employer complicates the financial working of schemes designed to counteract this evil.

The Briggs' experiment closed on the eve of the legislation which consolidated the status of the Trade Unions. Their development between that day and this makes it certain that they have come to stay, and that their function of collective bargaining is destined to be at least as important as that of their friendly benefits. It is to be suspected that in the 'sixties not a few employers and theorists welcomed profit-sharing as a means of knocking the bottom out of collective bargaining. James Nasmyth,[1] the master-engineer of steam-hammer

[1] *Cf.* his evidence before Royal Commission on Trades Unions, Qs. 19,095–19,340.

fame, spoke in eloquent praise of profit-sharing. " If there were more of that done it would result in great benefit individually and collectively to society. This method is the only way to deal with the present evil. It will come creeping on, for reason and justice are on its side, and when reason and justice are on the side of anything it will prevail." [1] He told the Royal Commission on Trade Unions how he had retired from business in 1856, ten years earlier than he would otherwise have done, such was the irritation of having to " walk on the surface of this continually threatening Trade Union volcano that was likely to burst out at every moment." He illustrated also his conception of the individual and collective benefit. He had started one of his workers on a single boring machine and finally put him in charge of six, raising his wage 1s. a time from 15s. to 21s.   " I do not mean to say that a shilling was a fair measure of the benefit that I got, but it was satisfactory to him and to me. . . . I was very niggardly in giving him only 21s. a week, but it is quite possible to spoil a man like that by giving him too much at once. . . . I should have liked to have tried the experiment, only the usual principle of business to get your work done as economically as possible deterred me, because any very unusual wages given

[1] Royal Commission on Trades Unions, Qs. 19,306–14.

to that man would soon have spread over the establishment."

It may be disputed whether in the last fifty years Trade Unions have been mainly responsible for the improvement in the position of wage earners as a whole, but in specific industries they have secured rises and prevented falls, and their value is so great as to make the substitution of Copartnership for Trade Unionism a thing neither to be expected nor desired. In the trades where Unionism is established, Copartnership must accommodate itself to the fact, and while leaving to the Unions the maintenance of the general minimum, con-centrate on the more equitable and harmonious distribution of the surplus above the minimum. This is the present policy of the businesses which are successfully practising Copartnership under these conditions. In spite of this accommodation, Copartnership is still mistrusted by the militant trade unionist. He is taught that the effectiveness of the peaceful pressure which he uses in the first instance, depends upon the preparedness of his instruments of war, and that, therefore, he should not acquiesce in a device like Copartnership under which these weapons will grow rusty.

The difficulties arising out of the complexities of company organisation and the assumptions of advanced unionism suggest to an unsympathetic mind the narrowing of Copartnership to industries where the Union has not yet appeared and to businesses in which the employer is a private individual. Copartnership would then be a pretty picture on a vanishing back-ground. The female employees of a benevolent patron cheer as their sisters are called up to receive a handshake and a postal order. Meanwhile, companies and men must struggle and lock-out and strike till the dawn of day or through eternal night; for some of the unsympathetic are in the ranks of socialism, and others are descended from Mr Nasmyth. Such a picture as this will not satisfy the advocates of Copartnership, who claim that their principle can be suitably applied in industries and businesses which are directly on the path of modern development. But it is well to see wherein the strength of their principle lies. For if regarded merely as a device of wage payment Copartnership or profit-sharing—it is then one and the same thing—has not very much to show. In the United Kingdom the Labour Copartnerships founded by workmen (the workers' productive societies) and the schemes of Copartnership instituted by employers have succeeded in adding to the wages of those affected an average bonus of $4\frac{1}{2}$ and $5\frac{1}{2}$ per cent. respectively between 1906 and 1910.[1] Five per cent. is not to

[1] Report on Profit-sharing and Labour Copartnership in the United Kingdom 1912. [Cd. 6496], pp. 16 and 82.

be despised, but after all it is only one-twentieth of the total. The formal weaknesses of profit-sharing as a method of remuneration are easy to expose. The workers are asked to make special efforts, and they are not secured in their reward for those efforts. Though they work ever so keenly, the year's operations may result in a loss as the result of financial conditions over which, as workers, they have no control.

There are forms of wage payment known to English readers as gain-sharing [1] which combine security of return with stimulus to effort. By these devices, the workers individually or in small groups receive, over and above their standard wage, extra rates or premiums for turning out work at less than standard cost and in less than standard time. They have only to make the extra effort in order to secure the extra reward, and they are not exposed to fluctuations resulting from misfortunes or mistakes in the general operation of the business. But even gain-sharing is not immune from a possible injustice. When the workers respond to the stimulus by rising above the standard, their action may be used as a lever for the subsequent raising of the standard itself. The old standard may be forgotten, and the workers may be asked to strain for their prize from an ever higher level.

[1] *Cf.* Report on Gain-sharing 1895. [Cd. 7848].

In a recent American work entitled "The Principles of Scientific Management," [1] the author, Mr F. W. Taylor, criticises devices like gain-sharing from the standpoint of employer and employed. He calls it the system of "incentive and initiative," in which "practically the whole of the problem is up to the workman," and contrasts it with the system of "scientific management"—successfully introduced by him into a large number of American establishments—in which "full one half of the problem is up to the management." [2]   Under this new system every workman in every process, however simple, whether it be carrying pig-iron, shovelling dust, or laying bricks, is minutely studied to the end that the rule of thumb may be replaced by the precision of science.   When by stop watches and calculating machines the management has ascertained the most that a man can do without injury to himself and the cheapest price at which an article can be turned out without loss of quality, then only can efficiency be expected and secured from the workers.   Each day's work for each man in the establishment is planned out in advance, and it is the function of the managers to see that everything happens according to plan.   "It is only through enforced standardisation of methods, en-

[1] Taylor's "Principles of Scientific Management," New York, 1911.
[2] *Ibid.*, p. 38.

forced adoption of the best implements and working
conditions, and enforced co-operation that this faster
work "—he is speaking of bricklaying at this point
—" can be assured." The results claimed are indeed
startling. Three hundred and fifty bricks per man
per hour, where some unions in the old countries
allow no more per day, and similar transformations
in other trades, with the joint result of a lower
labour cost for the employer and higher wages with
shorter hours for the workman. Wage increases
of 60 to 100 per cent. are given in evidence. We
shall not wonder that the author is scornful of
profit-sharing " either through selling stock to the
employees or through dividends on wages received
at the end of the year. . . . The nice time which they
[the men] are sure to have to-day, it they take things
easily and go slowly, proves more attractive than
steady hard work with a possible reward to be
shared with others six months later. . . . The few
misplaced drones who do the loafing and share
equally in the profits with the rest, under co-operation are sure to drag the better men down toward
their level." [1]   We can understand, too, that Mr
Taylor's subjects after an initial rebellion against the
new science soon yielded to its high rewards—a
doubling of wages and the sense of relief, altogether
new, at everything working out according to plan.

[1] Taylor, " Principles of Scientific Management," pp. 94-5.

But when the living machine is working with its full complement of fuel and the poignant contrast with the old disorder has died along with disorder itself, what then will remain ?   Leisure, the leisure of the free man will remain.   The worker, when he has passed outside the doors of the workshop, will woo culture in the long hours of recreation, and peradventure do homage to his industrial masters by the scientific management of the machine political.   " Now, one of the very first requirements," says Mr Taylor,[1] " for a man who is fit to handle pig iron as a regular occupation is that he shall be so stupid or so phlegmatic that he more nearly resembles in his mental make-up the ox than any other type."   Which occupant of the ark, we wonder, would supply the type of a Congressman?

But to scoff is easy.   For without doubt the champions of Copartnership have been guilty of underrating the possibilities of the ordinary wage relation.   It is no doubt often true that when gain-sharing or profit-sharing is first introduced the employers elicit a response from their men perhaps even to the extent of fully recouping themselves for the bonuses which they pay away.   But such responses are continually being elicited in ordinary businesses by improvements in workshop organisa-

[1] Taylor, " Principles of Scientific Management," p. 59.

B

tion and the elaboration of wage-rates on a piece-work basis, by greater discrimination in the allot-ment of duties and promotions to responsible posts, and by the introduction of new blood into the manage-ment itself. Though the remoter consequences of Mr Taylor's methods may appal us, yet they well suggest the power which is latent in the ordinary wage relation for the effective encouragement and reward of merit. If Copartnership is to be more than a display of fireworks fanned into brief brilliance by bonuses and good words, it must take its stand on wider ground and answer to deeper needs. It must not be simply an amended form of profit-sharing, but a larger whole in which profit-sharing with its possible shortcomings is a subordinate though essential part. It must spring from inten-tions which only stop at profit-sharing when technical exigencies for the time forbid further advance.

Generous members of the employing class may sometimes be heard to sigh for the family brother-hood that existed in the good old days of gilds and hard labour. Of these days Germany still retains some traces. She has done much by the organisation of co-operative credit to sustain and vitalise the small-scale industrialist. But whatever Germany's future may be, for England certainly there is no going back. No one who has read the death story of the handloom weavers in the grim evidence of Parliamentary Committee [1] and Royal Commission,[2] can wish to see the tragedy reopened. If the bond of union between the worker and his work is to be made more close, the means must be found nearer the lines along which our industrial evolution has run.

In the first half of the nineteenth century English democracy passed from infancy to adolescence. Political power preceded industrial emancipation. The spell of oligarchy was broken by two sharp strokes, the Reform Act of 1832 and the Municipal Corporations Act of 1834. What the middle classes won for themselves in the 'thirties, the course of later years has extended to the working population in town and country. Chartism at the time was a pitiable fiasco. But one by one the points of the Charter have been attained, or are within sight of approximate attainment. Property is still secure. The interest on the National Debt has not been repudiated. Society is not yet plunged in that chaos which, on Macaulay's augury,[3] was to be worse than the Siege of Jerusalem.

But the accommodation to industrialism was a task less easy. It is said that the school children in the South of England celebrated the victory of Waterloo by bearing round the town banners inscribed with

---

[1] 1834-5.   [2] 1839-41.
[3] Speech in the House of Commons, May 3, 1842.

the motto, "Peace and Plenty." Peace came but
no plenty, and the paradox staggered the friends of
the working man. In the camp and on the battle-
field there is a spirit of comradeship which calls out
mutual devotion and softens pain. This spirit found
no resting-place in England when it returned home
from the wars. Not that the face of England was cold
and dark—for the sky was bright at times with the
flames of burning hay-ricks, and bright every night
with the fires of the furnaces and with the gaslight
that spluttered inside the mills,—but the nation
itself was cold as stone, the rich from the bustle of
their riches and the poor from the long-drawn agony
of want. No Parliament of country gentlemen
or working men could have had the nerve to pass
the Poor Law Amendment Act of 1834. Philosophic
Radicals prepared the contents, and harassed shop-
keepers tied up the parcel with their stiffest string.

However, if the first work of the Reformed Parliament was to imprison the poor in workhouse Bastilles,
they subsequently did other and more fruitful work
by opening the eyes of the nation to a knowledge of
itself. The evidence of the various Committees and
Commissions appointed to inquire into the conditions of work in mills, mines, and workshops was
the necessary prelude to the effective code of factory
legislation which was obtained by Tory philan-
thropists and popular gatherings in the teeth of

opposition from Radical mill-owners, and the time-worn gospellers of Laissez-faire. But on the whole, apart from this, the legislators of the time lacked grip and breadth of outlook.

The little band of writers known as the Early English Socialists [1] faithfully reflect in themselves the merits and shortcomings of the age which they so severely condemned. They excelled in destructive criticism, but in construction they were weak and visionary. Their great right, the right of labour to the whole produce of labour, was at bottom individualistic, and like every gospel which speaks to the people altogether of rights and no whit of duties, it led them to nothing. Mazzini's impassioned wisdom, disclosed in the burning sentences of the " Duties of Man," [2] was justified of the early Socialists. After brilliantly exposing the seamy side of the classical political economy, they foundered on currency dodges and Utopias. Robert Owen was their master here, and unfortunately for them they followed their master in glorifying his visions and neglecting his earlier deeds.

[1] For their names and writings, see Anton Menger, "Right to the Whole Produce of Labour" (with introduction by Prof. H. S. Foxwell), London, 1899 ; and Esther Lowenthal, "The Ricardian Socialists," Columbia University, 1911.

[2] Joseph Mazzini, "On the Duties of Man" (1858). English edition published by the Copartnership Publishers, Ltd., with foreword by Henry Vivian.

For Robert Owen had done great things. Success-ful in an age when many were making fortunes, chivalrous in an age when calculation ruled supreme, Robert Owen had in early life built an edifice that was instinct with the spirit of Industrial Copartner-ship. From 1800 to 1819, in his cotton-mills at New Lanark on the Clyde, he was a model employer and a source of amazement to his work-people and the world at large. He reduced the hours of work, paid full wages and abstained from dismissals during a period of business stagnation, established a sick fund, a savings-bank, and a store which supplied the necessaries of life at wholesale prices, and built for the children of his workpeople a school in which he taught them by object-lesson, nature study, song, and dance. The workers re-sponded quickly. Drunkenness and illegitimacy, prevalent vices in the old days, disappeared, and all the while the business prospered. Owen's philosophy was a simple one. Environment is the cause of differences in character, and environment is under human control. If the care of inanimate machines yields such high profits, how much more will be yielded by the care of animate men and women ? But the adult cannot profit by this care unless as a child he is educated aright. Unfortu-nately, Owen's views on education brought him into conflict with the Church and the world of respecta-

bility, so that the benevolent, quixotic employer
of New Lanark, admired of princes and consulted
by Parliament, became the arch-heretic, the out-
cast, the father of Socialism. But outlawry only
increased his following by rallying to his side that
great section of the working class which was alive
to existing evils and passionately eager for emancipation. When he retired in disgust from the world
of Capitalism, he carried his disciples with him
whither he pleased.[1]

In 1821 a " Co-operative and Economical Society "
was formed in London, its ultimate object being
—to quote the constitution—" to establish a vil-
lage of unity and mutual co-operation, combining
agriculture, manufactures, and trades upon the plan
projected by Robert Owen." This opened the
era of Community Experiments, Orbiston in Scot-
land and a cluster of others in England, ending
with the Harmony Community, of which Owen was
for sometime the president, at Queenwood, Hamp-
shire. Their makers dreamed of a brotherhood of
freely associating individuals, rid of the oppressions
of Government and the frauds of competition ;
working for the joy of work, and playing with
orderly zeal ; pursuing agriculture where they would
see the whole process from the sowing of the seed

[1] For further details of Owen's career, see Frank Podmore's
" Robert Owen," 2 vols. 1906.

to the eating of the grain, and manufacturing with the aid of triumphant machinery the simple and useful products that would suffice for their maintenance. But the altruistic ardour of the townsmen was not equal to the successful conduct of rural economy, and bad cooking brought on indigestion, the parent of egoism.

However, it was in this rare atmosphere that the eminently solid Co-operative Movement was born.

> "Our cargo is Labour, our goal is the Land,
>   And Owen, our Captain, bids ALL heave a hand."

So the early co-operators sang. But to get the precious cargo into the promised land funds were necessary, and it was this necessity, not an appetite for dividend or a notion of organising industry from the standpoint of the consumer, that led to the establishment of the first co-operative stores. Owen either presided or assisted at the seven Co-operative Congresses held between May 1831 and March 1834 in Manchester, Birmingham, London (Gray's Inn Road), Liverpool, Huddersfield, London (Charlotte Street), and Barnsley respectively. He was a wayward president, urging the delegates at one time to establish communities, at another time to open labour bazaars; then to amalgmate with the Trades Unions, and finally to rally round himself in a "National Moral Union of the Productive Classes." Some sixty or seventy societies were represented at the earlier congresses, and at least a hundred more were reported to be working. Of those represented some had not got as far as trading, others were of the nature of workers' productive societies, and others again were mainly stores. The last sort often had in view the exchange of goods made by their own members with the products of other societies. The first outburst of Co-operation was short-lived. Of the 1421 co-operative stores existing in the United Kingdom in 1910, those established in this early period may be counted on the fingers. It was not till 1844 that the Rochdale Pioneers established their society on the lines since followed by the rest of England and most other countries of Europe. These lines are sale of goods at market prices, cash payment, and distribution of surplus profit among members proportionately to the amount of their purchases. But the connection between the old and the new Co-operation is visible in the first rules of the Rochdale Pioneers. The society's objects embraced the establishment of a store for the sale of provisions, clothing, etc., the building of houses for its members, the manufacture of such articles as would give employment to those of its members who were out of work or underpaid, a " self-supporting colony of united interests," and a Temperance Hotel.

The Act of 1862 gave co-operative societies the

precious boon of limited liability and facilitated the establishment of a wholesale society, composed of the stores themselves. Unsuccessful attempts in the latter direction had been made previously at Liverpool, London, and Rochdale ; but in 1863 the present English Wholesale Society was founded at Manchester, and in 1868 came the Scottish Wholesale Society at Glasgow. The English Wholesale began to manufacture for itself in 1873, and its Scottish sister soon followed suit. Almost insensibly both the stores themselves and the two Wholesales became great employers of labour. In 1911 they employed altogether nearly 74,000 persons in their distributive departments, and over 54,000 in their productive departments.

The earliest stores did not contemplate profit-sharing with their employees for the very good reason that profit was anathema to them. "Any trading societies," said the London Congress in 1832, "formed for the accumulation of profits with the view to merely making a dividend thereof at some future period cannot be recognised by this Conference as identified with the Co-operative world, nor admitted into that great social family which is now rapidly advancing to a state of in-dependent and equalised community."[1] After 1844, when the wisdom of the purchaser's dividend

---

[1] Quoted in C. Webb's "Industrial Co-operation," p. 58.

was brought home to them, many of the stores found it natural to associate their employees also in a share of the surplus profit. But to the distress of G. J. Holyoake and other veterans of the movement, profit-sharing with employees fell out of favour, with the result that in 1910 only 195 stores, approximately one in seven, followed this practice. The English Wholesale began profit-sharing in 1873, but in 1876 reported with dissatisfaction upon it, and, after another effort in 1882, abandoned it finally in 1886. Since 1907, however, the Society has had an Employees Thrift Fund to which the workers contribute a percentage on their wages and the Society itself adds a further but smaller percentage. The objects of the Fund are, " To make provision for the retirement of its members through old age or incapacity caused by infirmity of body or mind, the encouragement of thrift, and the creation of a bond of interest between the Society and Employees which shall be mutually advantageous." [1] The management of the Fund rests with a committee of eleven, six directors of the Society, and five elected employee members, who together are trustees for the investment of the Funds (in 1910, £88,390) with the Wholesale Society.

The Scottish Wholesale Society has pursued a

[1] Board of Trade Report on Profit Sharing and Labour Copartner ship, 1912, p. 78.

different policy. It began profit-sharing in 1870, and has continued it ever since. From 1892 one-half of each worker's bonus has been retained in a Bonus Loan Fund, carrying 3 per cent. interest, and withdrawable only on retirement. In the same year the employees were given power to hold shares in the Society, and they are entitled to send one representative to the General Meetings, with an additional representative for every 150 employees who become shareholders. No employee, however, can hold any office on the Committee of Management or be an auditor of the Society. At the end òf 1910 561 out of 7611 employees were shareholders, and as such entitled to four votes at the shareholders' meetings.[1]

The historian of Co-operation must find it difficult to pronounce between these two policies. If the one may claim adherence to the early notion of no profits, the other seems more in keeping with the early spirit of co-operative fellowship. But the presence or absence of profit-sharing in co-operative stores, retail or wholesale, cannot be considered to indicate a fundamental divergence in the movement at the present time. The real difference is between Co-operation fifty years ago and Co-operation to-day. Then the employees were few, one or two to each shop ; now they are numerous, even in a single

[1] Board of Trade Report on Profit Sharing and Labour Copartnership, 1912, p. 78.

store. Then the stores produced practically nothing for themselves ; now the bigger ones have productive departments of their own, and the several factories of the Wholesale Society employ hundreds, in some cases one or two thousand workers, under a single roof. It may be allowed that the co-operative store has done great and revolutionary things for the organisation of working-class consumption, but it is also true that as an employer of labour it has been content with the wage relation that prevails in ordinary industry. That surplus of which Herman Merivale spoke in 1868 is not abolished by the co-operative store within the sphere of its operations. It is merely distributed in countless rills to purchasing numbers in proportion to the assistance they give in making it. Like the managers of any public company, the managing committees of the co-operative stores have to reconcile the interests of their members with the distinct interests of their wage-earning employees, and in comparison with the public company they have only this one advantage that being themselves working men, or the delegates of working men, they should be alert to satisfy the just claims of fellow-workers.

In the villages of medieval England production and consumption were not sharply differentiated. Somewhat similarly, in the first phase of industrial Co-operation, the elements of production and consumption were not separated, being fused in the white heat of ideal communion. But when the stores developed on business lines and so attained to national proportions (for idealism is particular and languishes in the mass), the transformation of the wage system passed out of the Co-operative programme. In 1850-52 Vansittart Neale, Thomas Hughes, and their co-workers among the Christian Socialists conducted a Society for the Promotion of Working Men's Associations, and set up or encouraged a number of small self-governing workshops which for various reasons—over-assistance, isolation, and want of funds—soon came to an end. Further independent endeavours followed, and the failures were again very numerous. In 1884, however, there was formed the body which now bears the name of the Labour Copartnership Association,[1] and since that time workers' productive societies have grown in number and met with striking success. In 1910 [2] eighty of these workers' societies were doing a trade of nearly 1½ millions sterling per annum. Some of them, among which is the Walsall Locks and Cart-Gear Society, founded as far back as 1873, produce for the open market, but the majority of the bigger societies sell most or all of their output to the

[1] London offices, 6 Bloomsbury Square, W.C.
[2] *Cf.* Report on Industrial and Agricultural Co-operative Societies in the United Kingdom, 1912 [Cd. 6045] xxx.—xxxii., etc.

co-operative stores. The workers' societies of the
latter order are none the less independent societies.
The capital is provided in part by the workers
themselves and in part by co-operative stores and
persons interested in this side of the co-operative
movement. The interest on capital is a first charge
on profit and usually limited to 5 per cent., and a
part at least of the surplus profit is allotted to the
workers proportionately to their wages. Where the
stores are themselves big customers, the rules of the
society sometimes assign them a dividend on purchases parallel with the workers' dividend on wages.

The constitution of the workers' societies is thus
a mixed one. The workers founded the societies,
the stores backed them up with capital and custom.
The workers have their own representatives on the
committee of management, while the existence
of other share-holders, whether represented on the
committee or not, corrects any tendency to one-
sidedness and makes it easier for the manager to
exercise that full authority which is necessary to
the successful execution of business enterprise.
The stores offer a good market, but a market which
is not guaranteed. The workers' societies have to
compete with the productive departments of the
Wholesale Society and with outside competition
as well. A rivalry between the workers' societies
and the Wholesale is a healthy stimulus to both

parties, and it operates in the area in which the co-operative stores are furthest removed from the checks of market-price. The workers' societies are strongest in the textile and leather trades, clothing and boots being in constant demand by the stores. The Midlands district about Kettering and Leicester seems to possess an atmosphere congenial to Labour Copartnership. One success helps to another, but its peculiar strength in the boot trade suggests that the technique of the industry is exceptionally amenable to democratic organisation. It has been suggested that the gaps between the different grades from the least skilled man to the top are not great in the boot trade, and that this enables the workers to understand different processes and thereby to make an intelligent use of their influence in the control of the business. There seems to be no hostility between the trade unions and the workers' societies, and there is no ground for any. The members are generally union men, working standard hours and drawing standard pay.

It is not a matter for surprise that these little industrial republics increase but slowly. In the first place the members set out to do a very difficult thing, namely, to work in a factory at the orders of their manager and at the same time to sit at the committee table by this same manager's side. The manager appoints his foreman from among the best brains in the place, and perhaps would like to see a larger number of them on the committee of management. For it is only natural that when the worker comes to voting he should prefer to the foreman under whom he works all day long some one rather closer to himself in outlook and status. In the second place, the workers' society cannot easily add an outside trade to a nucleus of store custom. For " the trade " still dislikes Co-operation and everyone who touches it or bears the name. The knowledge or suspicion that a workers' society does business with the co-operative stores may cause it to be refused, or to lose, outside custom. Buyers who would prefer to look only to the quality of the out-put may be subjected to pressure from trade producers.

Finally, most of these societies are still in their youth. The young men who founded them are now mature workers, and one day they must retire. When a man can no longer work the full pace the ordinary employer discharges him, unless he is exceptional, and leaves him to provide for himself. A workers' society cannot but shrink from applying this drastic policy to its own seniors, to the men whose spirit created the business and carried it through its early trials. Yet the business must keep strong and up-to-date on pain of failure. Something may be done by allowing the manager ample discretion in setting

c

the older men to suitable work paid at less than standard rates. Certain of the larger societies are wisely looking ahead, and reserving part of their profits for the establishment of funds out of which provision is being made for retirement through accident and old age.

We have travelled up and down the century in our quest for the genius of Copartnership. We began on orthodox lines, shed a tear over Briggs' colliery, and wondered whether profit-sharing after all was so admirable a thing. We then took a wider view and plunged with seeming irrelevance into politics, bewildered by the paradox that as the avenue was opened to the privileges of active citizenship, the door seemed to shut more closely than ever on that other form of patriotism, the patriotism of the workshop. For a moment we thought to take our stand at New Lanark. But the elusive spirit lured us to the land, and we might as well have gone to the unemployment colony at Hollesley Bay. For industrialism cannot be solved in the fields, nor is the salvation of agriculture to be found on the path of industry. To appreciate the significance of Copartnership in agriculture we should have to compare the relation of landlord and tenant in England with the Metayer system of Latin Europe, and ask whether the fixed rental of English tenancy does not result in more fruitful

collaboration than the formal sharing of a part of
the produce. And perhaps we might conclude
that in some departments of agriculture that system
is the best in which no need for a division of claims
arises, in which, in fact, small men owning or secured
in the tenancy of their farms work the land mainly
with their own labour, and join together for the
purchase of materials and the disposal of produce.
But our concern is with industry, and we leave
agriculture with a single observation. Co-operative
dairies, jointly owned by farmers, have employees,
and some of the co-operative dairies in Ireland
associate their employees in a share of the profits.

There remained the great commonwealth of the
co-operative stores, with its 2¾ million members.
Could we not say to our spirit, " We can do without
you : here is a great federation of consumers which
has pushed backwards from retailing to wholesale,
from wholesale to manufacture, from manufacture
to shipping and agricultural exploits in Great
Britain, Ireland, and Ceylon ? " ¹   No ; the store
structure is unsuited to agriculture just because
agriculture is agriculture : and in industry we have
already seen the point at which the solution of the
store stops short, at the point, namely, of the labour
problem. From the high call which they make on

¹ Board of Trade Report on Profit-Sharing and Labour Copartnership, 1912, p. 86.

the imagination and restraint of their members as well as from their connection with the co-operative stores, the workers' societies operate in restricted fields and increase but slowly in number. Thus we are brought back to our starting-point, to the great world of ordinary business. Does this world need to be transformed ? Can Copartnership transform it ? To the first question we plead an ignoramus, to the second we attempt an answer in the pages which follow.

Copartnership is very much in the air to-day, in fact there is a boom in the theory of it. But an ounce of accomplishment is worth a ton of good intentions ; and success is as hard as failure is easy. Some schemes miscarry because the business itself is unsuccessful or because the workers decline the experiment : others fail from inherent weakness. Those which have succeeded have been conceived by men of an original and generous mind, and if they are to last they will require from the succeeding generation a steady adherence to the high standard set by the founders. " Omnia praeclara tam difficilia quam rara sunt," said Spinoza. " All things excellent are as difficult as they are rare." Peradventure, this is not less true of industry than of philosophy.

CHAPTER II

ECONOMICS and politics are nearly related, albeit
the connection is not to be forced by applying the
jargon of economics to the greater subtleties of
government. English students, however, are prone
to neglect the inter-relation. For our economists
know no law, our lawyers are peculiarly specialised,
and our historians are rather proud of not possessing economic minds. Furthermore, in England,
economic stress has rarely precipitated political
catastrophe, and in recent times under a temperate
form of government great latitude has been extended
to economic experiments by private persons and
bodies. Our law has been negligently kind to
novelties and has gracefully confirmed the Company
and Trust in the sweeping domain carved out by
themselves. If one arm of the trust has reached
in America to industrial combination and thus by
accident given to combination a title which is now
meaningless, another arm in England has been felt
by the wage-earners in a very different way. Trustees
protect the interests of the workers in the most

successful Copartnerships and one of these schemes is officially styled a Copartnership Trust.

But in France, from the course of French history and the mould of French life, politics and economics have been closely interwoven ; and all forms of economic association have been forbidden or jealously confined by a government imbued with the individualist principles of the Revolution of 1789. This interweaving of interests and this policy of government have left their marks on Copartnership in France.

GODIN

Jean-Baptiste André Godin died on January 15, 1888, aged 71, at Guise, in the department of Aisne, in the north of France. His work remains to-day the same in form as he left it at the moment of his death. The original statutes [1] of Godin's Association or Copartnership bear the date 1880 ; and Section II. of these runs as follows : " The Association between workers and capitalists founded at the Familistère of Guise on the initiative of M. Godin takes the name of the Society of the Familistère of Guise, Co-operative Association of Capital and

[1] Printed in full in Godin's " Mutualité Sociale," and covering about 150 pages. For a general account see "Twenty-eight Years of Co-partnership at Guise," translated from the French of M. Prudhom-meaux and others by Aneurin Williams: London, 1908.

Labour, under the style of Godin & Co. . . . The Association aims at the organisation of solidarity among its members through the participation of capital and labour in the profits . . . It purposes to carry on the affairs of the Familistère together with its shops and stores, likewise the business of the workshops and foundries belonging to the Founder and situated at Guise and at Laeken-lez-Bruxelles." The latter is the branch establishment in Belgium, much smaller in size but operated on precisely the same lines as the parent association. The works and the Familistère in which the workers dwell adjoin each other. " Poêles Godin," or Godin's stoves, is a notice familiar to the traveller entering France. In addition to stoves and other apparatus for heating and cooking, the works turn out baths, cisterns, and a multitude of small articles, braziers, inkstands, and the like. Much of the work is heavy, requiring strength and some skill. The workers number over 2000, 1600 at Guise and 500 at Schaerbeck (formerly called Laeken), and of this total under 100 are women. The dwellings of the Familistère are situated across the way in an arm of the river Oise. The visitor, as he comes from the centre of the town, passes by the theatre, library, and schools of the Society, into an open square where the statue of Godin stands, and sees before him three blocks of dwellings containing interior courts roofed in glass. Close by are two further blocks built later than the rest (for the common dwellings are much sought after), while kitchen gardens and a small park and a terrace of flower-beds form a pleasing back-ground to the whole. The buildings accommodate 1800 persons, of whom 500 are employed in the works, and the remainder are women and children and other domestic dependents. Only some third, therefore, of the workers inhabit the common dwellings, the other two-thirds living outside in the town.

The Society is by law " *en commandite simple,*" *i.e.* one with limited liability. Godin directed the Society up to the time of his death. Mme. Godin succeeded him for the next six months, when she retired in favour of M. Dequenne, who in turn in 1897 was succeeded by the present manager, M. Colin. The manager directs both the works and the Familistère. He is assisted in both tasks by a Council of Management comprising the heads of departments and three representatives of the working members of the Society. In business matters the Council is advisory only, but in other directions it has executive power. For the ordinary routine of business the Council meets under another name, the Council of Industry, while for the internal administration of the Familistère those members of the Council of Management who have the status of

Associé meet as the Council of the Familistère. The powers of the manager are very full, especially on the business side, although, of course, he is bound by the statutes of Association. Elected for life by the General Assembly, he may be dismissed by it if he violates the constitution, or is privately interested in its transactions, or involves it in losses over £2000 against the advice of the Council of Management and the General Assembly. Finally, a Council of Supervision, though technically improper to a society *en commandite*, holds a watching brief for the General Assembly.

This General Assembly is the statutory sovereign. None but workers are members of it, and none of the workers not members of it have a voice in the policy of the Society. Its functions are to elect representatives to the above mentioned councils, to admit qualified candidates to its own ranks, to receive from the manager the annual statements of the Society's progress, and on extraordinary occasions, when requested by the manager, to advise on general policy. The Society, however, is wider than the General Assembly, which is, as it were, the inner temple of the building. For the society has four classes of members :—1. Associés ; 2. Sociétaires ; 3. Participants ; 4. Interessés. The terms have a technical significance, and may be best translated 1st class, 2nd class, 3rd class, 4th class members.

The 4th class members (interessés) may be briefly dismissed. They are defined as "persons who are members of the Association solely because they are, by inheritance or in any other way, shareholders."[1] They get interest on their capital, but no share in profits beyond the fraction allotted to the dividend on capital, and they have no say in the Society's affairs. In this class come the beneficiaries under Godin's will and ex-members of the Society or their descendants, whose shares are not yet paid out.

The 1st class members constitute the aforesaid General Assembly. To qualify for 1st class membership a worker must have worked for the Society and have lived in the Familistère at least five years, and he must hold £20 of the Society's capital. A 1st class member who is forced to retire from active service by reason of old age or sickness may continue to live in the Familistère and vote at the General Assembly.

The 2nd and 3rd class members are chosen from the remaining body of the workers by the managers and Council of Management. They must have worked for the Society a minimum of three years and one year respectively. Residence in the Familistère is compulsory for the 2nd class and optional for the 3rd.

In addition to these four classes, and outside the Society, is an extra class of *Auxiliaires* or helpers,

[1] Article 29 of the Statutes.

composed of the new hands and floating population of the works. In 1899 the membership of the Society was distributed as follows [1] :—

Active members of Class I. (*associés*) .	316
,, ,, ,, II. (*sociétaires*) .	160
,, ,, ,, III. (*participants*) .	615
Holders of savings certificates no longer working for the Society [2] . .	502
	1593
Helpers (*auxiliaires*)	795
	2388

With this may be compared the composition of the Society at the outset in 1880 :—

Class I.	46
Class II.	62
Class III.	442
	550

Membership in the 2nd class was intended by Godin to be a stepping-stone to the tried ranks of full 1st class membership, and it has been so employed. But the 3rd class is separated from the 2nd not so much by the qualification of age and experience as by that of residence ; and this would

[1] *Cf.* "Notice sur la Société du Familistère," 1900, p. 29.

[2] See below, pp. 45-7.

seem to be an element of weakness. For from limitations of space many workers cannot, and from personal preference some workers do not, enter the Familistère. Hence, much of the dwelling-space of the Familistère is unavoidably occupied by the resident workers' families, some members of which are perhaps employed in the town, and at the same time there are living in the town experienced workers of Class III., whose presence at the General Assembly and its adjuncts would promote the Society's welfare. It may be remarked that out-dwelling members of Class III. who have worked for the Society twenty years are given a share in the profits equal to that of Class II.[1]

The distribution of profits accords with the constitution of the Society, and is regulated with ingenious precision. Deductions in cash from the gross profits are first of all made on account of depreciation of buildings and plant, votes to the various mutual assurance funds, the expenses of education, and the payment of a fixed interest at 5 per cent. on the whole of the share capital. The surplus profit remaining is distributed—

75 per cent. to " Capital and Labour."
25 per cent. to " Ability."

Of the 25 per cent, 4 per cent. goes to the manager,

[1] But see Appendix I., p. 139.

16 per cent. to the different managing Councils, 2 per cent. to the Council of Inspection, 2 per cent. to the reward of signal services, and 1 per cent. towards maintaining in national schools boys and girls who have already passed through the school of the Familistère. Apart from this, the manager receives a fixed salary of £600, which is rather less than the average equivalent of his 4 per cent. share in profits. Godin, like Schulze-Delitzsch, believed that every form of useful work should be remunerated, and therefore allotted fees for attendance at the meetings of the councils. The 2 per cent. for signal services is distributed by the Council of Management among workers who suggest improvements and economies.

It was, however, in the allocation of the 75 per cent. to Capital and Labour that Godin's imagination was most fertile and courageous. Godin held that the 5 per cent. paid to Capital as its just and sufficient wage must be the measure of its share in the surplus profit. " Labour's part," says Article 128 of the Statutes, " is represented by the total of earnings for the year, and Capital's part by the total of interest payments for the year. Capital's part is payable in cash and Labour's part in Savings Certificates "—the nature of which we shall explain in a moment. By calculating on the interest of Capital instead of on the Capital sum itself, Godin very materially reduced the size of the second payment to Capital. The workers' share is allotted in proportion to their earnings, with the further modification that for the reckoning of individual shares the quotas of 1st and 2nd Class members are multiplied by 2 and 1½ respectively.

When Godin established his Association in 1880 he did not give his property to the workers, and yet the workers as a society are the legal owners of the property to-day. The workers bought out Godin, and yet no levy was ever made on their wages for this purpose. How was this possible ? The purchase money came from the workers' share of profits, and in 1894 the lengthy process of buying out the founder was completed. By this date Godin or his representatives [1] had received a sum of £184,000, the original unimproved value of the property ; and the workers had accumulated an equivalent total of savings certificates, on each portion of which from the respective dates of accrual, they had been drawing in cash 5 per cent. interest and a fraction of further dividend. The founder's claims having now been satisfied, it would have been financially possible henceforth to pay out Labour's share of the profit in cash. But this step, by fixing

---

[1] When Godin died in 1888, he left by his will one half of his personal fortune—the maximum which French law gave him power to dispose of—to the Society. Therefore, to the extent of this one half, the Society received a further capital endowment.

the ownership of the capital in the hands of the workers who happened to constitute the Society in 1894 would have defeated Godin's end : and Godin, accordingly, had provided against it in the terms of Association. Since 1894 the workers have continued to receive their annual profits in the form of savings certificates, and the funds thus set at liberty are used to pay off the certificates of retired members. Thus each worker, while a worker, is allotted certificates proportionately to his earnings, and each worker on retirement is, as the profits of the Society permit, paid out in cash. This was a brilliant device, securing that each generation of workers should own the property of the Society, so long as they were active members of it and gradually realise the value of their holding at the close of their working life. Individuals come and go, but the body endures.

The corporate impress is further deepened by the common dwellings of the Familistère and the various schemes of mutual assurance. The residents rent from the Society their separate apartments or, as we should call them, flats. On the ground floor of the dwellings they have their shops, which though for fiscal reasons not registered as co-operative associations are in fact co-operative stores of the English type. The Society provides the capital for the stores, and hands over 85 per cent. of the surplus

profit for distribution to purchasers proportionately
to their purchases. The dividends, paid in credits
and converted ultimately into goods, were in 1906-7
at the rate of 2s. in the £1 on purchases and in total
they were approximately equal to the rental which
the inhabitants of the Familistère paid for their
apartments. The expenses of the nursery attached
to the Familistère, as also the expenses of its school,
theatre, and other places of study and recreation,
are met by the prior charges on the general funds
of the Society.

The mutual assurance funds embrace everybody.
We have already mentioned the extra class of
helpers (*auxiliaires*) 795 in all, who are not members
of the Society, and have no individual share in the
profits. Had Godin no thought for these ? Did he
perhaps, without intending it, create an aristocracy
of workers having under them a class of unbenefited
inferiors ? No ; he took thought for everybody.
Not only are the helpers, as soon as they become
permanent, eligible for membership in the Society ;
not only are they, when space permits, admitted
to live in the Familistère ; but also they are from
their entry into the works associated in the several
schemes of mutual assurance. A share in the profits
is assigned to the helpers, but as they are not of the
the Society, their share is paid into the Pensions
and Necessities Fund.

This fund is financed by a charge on the income of the Society prior to any distribution of profits. The charge is equal to 3 per cent. of the Society's wage bill, and the pensions provided for retired workers range from £14 to £36 per annum. In addition, the Society draws on the fund for special money grants to necessitous families, the head of the family being in no circumstance allowed to sell or pawn his savings certificates. No one in the Society and no one connected with it by ties of family and work can ever fall into the situation in which relief is needed and not forthcoming. To all members of Classes I. and II. and to their families, as also (if the Managing Council thinks fit) to 3rd Class members and helpers and their families a minimum of subsistence is guaranteed at the rate of 2s. per day for adults and at lower rates for widows, young persons, and children. Out of another fund, to which the workers contribute 1 to 1½ per cent. of their wages and the Society adds an equal sum, provision is made in cases of sickness or accident. The whole of this assurance work is managed by committees of workers under the supervision of the Managing Council and the members of the committees, in accordance with Godin's principle, are remunerated for their work.[1]

Thus the Association of Guise is at once a business and a family, the one being complementary to the

[1] See also the end of Appendix I., p. 139.

D

other. The workers in the family are arranged into grades, but the divisions are not abrupt and impassable. A minority only of the members has a voice in the Society's policy, but there is an open way into the ranks of the minority, and by means of the various forms of assurance the helpers are made to feel that they, too, have their recognised place in the scheme of Association.

STATISTICS

A. Profits—

75% OF THE PROFITS ARE ALLOTTED TO THE WAGES OF LABOUR AND THE INTEREST OF CAPITAL

	Profits to divide.	Total allotted to Wages.	Total allotted to the Interest of Capital.	Sum total allotted to Wages and the Interest of Capital.
1879-80 .	£17,181	£10,065	£1,389	£11,454
1889-90 .	13,470	9,343	759	10,102
1899-1900	17,452	11,881	808	12,689
1909-10 .	30,260	20,018	1,228	21,246
Total, 30 years	£497,655	£338,484	£26,952	£365,436

25% OF THE PROFITS ARE ALLOTTED TO ABILITY.

	To Managing Director.	To Councils of Management and Supervision.	Maintenance of Children in Government Schools.	Rewards for useful Inventions.
1879-80	£2,749	£2,520	..	£458
1889-90	538	2,020	134	269
1899-1900	698	2,504	174	349
1909-10	1,210	4,454	302	605
Total, 30 years	£30,682	£71,064	£4,026	£10,479

B. *Assurance Funds—*

| | | Sickness. | | | Retiring Pensions. | | |
| | | Men. | | Women. | | | |
	Receipts.	Payments.	Receipts.	Payments.	Pensions.	No. of Pensioners.	Average Pension.
1879-80 . .	£1,221	£1,011	£166	£133	£260	9	£28
1889-90 . .	1,199	1,405	302	300	1,753	67	26
1899-1900 .	1,492	1,469	328	440	3,767	135	27
1909-10 . .	2,343	2,146	332	298	4,917	164	29
Total 30 years,	£50,541	£50,358	£9,067	£9,131	£80,856	..	..

PAYMENTS FOR—I. NECESSITIES OF SUBSISTENCE, AND II. ANALOGOUS PURPOSES.

| | I. | | II. | |
		Families Helped.		Persons Helped.
1879-80 . .	£196	17	£180	22
1889-90 . .	536	43	233	42
1899-1900 .	508	46	297	42
1909-10 . .	845	69	516	66
Total, 30 years	£15,103	..	£12,116	..

Godin had read widely in the social literature of his generation, and he was himself no mean writer. An absolute democrat, and owning an even more unconditioned obedience than Rousseau himself to natural justice and the rights of man, he had little sympathy with the despotic hierarchy of Saint-Simon. Nevertheless, he endeavoured to extract a meaning from the formula *à chacun selon sa capacité, à chaque*

capacité suivant ses œuvres : which he interpreted
as discrimination in appointments and precise correspondence between work and wages. Any aspirant
to a post, says Article XII. of the rules of association, may submit a note to the manager in which
he states—(1) his conception of the post to which
he aspires in regard to the interests of the Association
and the advancement of the industry, and (2) the
improvement which he thinks possible in the post
he already holds. One of Godin's earliest reforms
in the then minute foundry at Guise was to replace
time wages by piece rates, and in Article XVII. of
the rules he draws the attention of members to the
fact that they had an interest in a just and precise
correspondence between work and wages inasmuch
as " profits, if any, are to be divided in proportion
to the labour rendered by each."

Godin's intellectual master was Charles Fourier,
the lonely little clerk from Marseilles, pale, passionate,
absorbed in the vision of his cosmic harmonies,
laughed at by common-sense critics, and revered
by men of imagination and heart. For was it not
Fourier himself who said—we paraphrase his words
—" but what matter these accessories beside the
main business which is the art of organizing industry
so that good habits may be established, harmony
may reign between rich, middle-class, and poor,
pestilence, revolution, and poverty may cease, and

the strife of parties may be resolved in universal unity ? " In Fourier's vision Godin found his ideal of social harmony—consumption correlated with production, the ordered leisure of the Phalanstery in congruity with the ordered joy of work. The same gospel which lured Louis Blanc to the fiasco of the National Workshops inspired the triumph of the Familistère. From Fourier Godin derived his formula of partition between Labour, Capital, and Talent, like Fourier he reverenced women and loved the little children. "Harmony," said Fourier, "will not commit the folly of excluding women from medicine and education, and of relegating them to the needle and the kitchen." The Society of the Familistère includes both men and women among its 1st class members, and the Pensions Committee is composed of eighteen members, nine men and nine women. And if Fourier could visit Guise to-day, how he would rejoice to talk with the good-looking dame who tends the infants in the nursery of the Familistère !

As one traverses the courts of the Familistère or passes through the workshops, one is forced to the thought that here the social problem simply does not exist. But it did exist once. Godin was an extraordinary man dealing with very ordinary men and women, and it took him his whole long career to call into being the corporate life which has survived him. He began business at Guise in 1846, during the next few years raised wages, shortened hours, and started assurance funds. In 1859 he laid the first stone of the Familistère. In 1876 the Association was founded in fact, and on August 13, 1880, it was clothed in legal solemnity. Eight years after Godin died. The decade from 1867 to 1878 was devoted to the work of social experiment,[1] which was momentarily interrupted by the national tragedy of the Franco-German war. In the disastrous months of 1870-71 Godin, first as chairman of the Town Council and then as Mayor of Guise, rendered heroic services to his town and country. The war ended, he returned to his unfinished work. With the literalness characteristic of his nature, he experimented on his workers in order to ascertain whether a voting democracy could control an industry as fitly as it could control national policy. The office staff and a number of picked workers were grouped now as a single electoral body, now in small bodies, now in bodies with several stages of election, and were invited each year from 1870 to 1872 to distribute certain moneys among the workpeople in proportion to merit. Godin found that the electorate, however arranged, either scattered its votes in a spirit of charity or concen-

[1] *Cf.* J. Prudhommeaux, "Les Expériences Sociales de J.-B. A. Godin" (1867-1878). Nimes, 1911.

trated them on friends. Then in 1872 he asked first a very limited electorate and afterwards the whole body of the Familistère to arrange a selected number of workers in order of merit, and distribute prizes among them. Of the selected group 103 had been nominated by himself, but alas! in the voting 55 of his nominees were blackballed. We smile; Godin persevered. In 1877, when the Association was coming into being, he instituted a further series of experiments designed to train the workers for their industrial democracy. This time all the workers and the residents in the Familistère were invited to divide themselves into groups of study; 162 groups in all corresponding to the 162 categories of work in the Society, each person being allowed to join as many as he liked. The groups were organised in a hierarchy—group, union of groups, sub-council, general council. "The mission of the groups," said Godin, " is simply a mission of examination and study. When its opinion has passed through this hierarchy, it will arrive finally at myself, and there receive, if suitable, practical acknowledgment. Thus a moral evolution will work in your minds [1] . . . Under the small master the family group in its entirety applies itself to the work of production, in the Association it will be the group

[1] "Documents pour une biographie complète de J.-B. A. Godin," par sa veuve, née Marie Moret, vol. iii. p. 64.

which will endow each one of the workers with the
spirit of initiative and liberty of action with which
the small artizan was equipped . . ." [1] After a
year or two the grandiose project fell through, the
causes which paralysed it being " above all, the
insufficiency and inertia of those concerned."
Though 2½d. was paid for each attendance, only
33 per cent. of the men and 4½ per cent. of the
women ever joined at all. The groups which met
did in some cases produce reports, which in Godin's
opinion embodied serviceable suggestions. But in
the sum Godin had ruefully to confess that the
workers, even the better among them, were not yet
fitted to adjudge awards or to plan out the processes
of industry. A better result at this time could
hardly have been expected by anyone less sanguine
than Godin. Many of the workers were illiterate,
many thought that the sharing of profits concealed
some fraud, and had indeed at first declined it;
some of the workers knowing that the founder's son [2]
was far from sharing his father's views, thought to
gain the son's favour by holding aloof. Not till
1894 when the savings certificates of retiring workers
began to be paid out in cash, were the rank and file

[1] "Documents pour une biographie complète de J.-B. A. Godin,"
par sa veuve, née Marie Moret, vol. iii. p. 124.

[2] Godin's only son was born in 1840, and died in 1888, a fortnight
before his father : he left a widow and children, the heirs by law of one-
half of Godin's fortune. The son separated from the father in 1878,

quite convinced that there was not an hallucination somewhere.

Godin was a member of the National Assembly from 1871 to 1876. In 1878 he founded *Le Devoir*, a monthly review of social questions, the publication of which was continued till 1906, and some years later a Society for Peace and International Arbitration. In 1883 he published his most mature work, " Government, or True Socialism in Action." The book closes with the draft of a bill, proposing that the State should succeed to the real and personal property of all persons having no direct or testamentary heir. and should impose on all other property a death duty of from 1 per cent. to 50 per cent., according to the size of the estate. The funds were to be employed in the remission of indirect taxation and in the provision of national insurance against old age, sickness, and want. In this way, he contended, the State might achieve on a national scale the reforms which he had effected at Guise. But with that strange mixture of idealism and statesmanship which is his peculiar charm, he called upon the State not indeed to compel imitations of himself, but to exact by taxation what he had given, or rather rendered, to his workpeople at Guise. "Nul n'est absolument propriétaire de ce qui est l'œuvre de la nature et des progrès antérieurs de la société."[1] This he

---

[1] "Le Gouvernement," p. 433.

believed : therefore the Familistère : therefore the project of law. The anti-socialist union in England has already published one pamphlet on Copartnership   Godin's work at Guise in relation to Godin's project of law for France would make good material for a second.

LECLAIRE

Edme-Jean Leclaire [1] house-painter of Paris, was born in May 1801 and died in July 1872.   He lived to the same age as Godin, but was his senior by sixteen years. The two men were cast in a very different mould. The benevolent bearded face of Godin contrasts with Leclaire's quiet, clean-shaven outlines. Godin's tongue was as eloquent as his pen. He loved to address his people at their annual Labour Festivals, and to see his ideas growing up around him in bricks and mortar. We may be sure he would have welcomed the notion of his statue standing in the square which contains the Familistère. Leclaire, to the last, found writing difficult. When a friend once corrected for him the grammar of a sentence, he retorted with characteristic vivacity, " Mais, monsieur, vous dénaturez ma pensée : je me . . . moque du français." Some years before his death, Leclaire's workers desired a medallion of their

---

[1] *Cf.* Charles Robert, " Biographie d'un homme utile : Leclaire." Paris, 1878.

master.   A skilled artist was placed in ambush to
make the sketch, and when Leclaire detected the ruse,
he with difficulty repressed an outburst of anger.

Godin lived out in the provinces, which are so very
different from the capital, and there he could imagine
himself creating a community more successful than
Victor Considérant's ill-starred venture in Texas, in
which he had in earlier days lost £4000.   Leclaire
worked in Paris with the atmosphere of Paris about
him, painting now for private clients and now for
public authorities, and basing his wages rate on the
tariff of the public works department of the municipality.   He had to interfere with Government only
for the reason that Government interfered with him.
He was studiously careful that each step in his profit-
sharing scheme should conform to the law and be
duly registered.   There is still extant the police
report of September 21, 1843, which says : " It will be
a danger for the working classes and an abuse, to
authorise the reunions of the workmen of the Sire
Leclaire, painting contractor, to concert upon the distribution of the profits accruing from the business."

Nevertheless, Leclaire and Godin both drew their
inspiration from the same central source.   " *Ah !
frappe-toi le cœur : c'est là qu'est le génie.*"   Godin
tells us [1] how, when he had left his father's shop on
his journeyman's tour and was working day after

[1] "Solutions Sociales," p. 14.

day from 5 A.M. to 8 P.M., he vowed to himself,
" If ever I rise above the condition of a worker, I
will seek a way to make his life less intolerable and
hard, and to elevate the labour that now bows him
down." Leclaire, in turn a shepherd-boy, a mason,
and a harvester, went to Paris and became by chance
a painter's apprentice. In 1827 he was in business
for himself, and in 1838 he erected the first storey of
his edifice of Copartnership, the Mutual Aid Society,
limited at the outset to a portion of the workers.
When in 1842 he proposed profit-sharing, he had to
meet, in addition to police obstruction, the mistrust
of his men and the denunciations of the working-
class press. " Will the money really be paid ? "
asked the men. Leclaire summoned them, placed
a bag of money on the table, and handed to each his
share. Opposition from within disappeared. The
working-class press constantly accused Leclaire of
manœuvring to lower wages. As late as 1876, four
years after Leclaire's death, a reporter to the working-
men's delegation at the Philadelphia Exhibition
said, " not to speak, not to drink, not to smoke " (he
was quoting from the rules)—" why! this house treats
its workers almost as if they were slaves, prisoners,
martyrs. . . . Profit-sharing creates a category of
contented beings who will prevent their comrades
from solving the social question by the Association
of Production." Had he been reporting thirty years

later he would have said, " by the nationalization
of the instruments of production, distribution, and
exchange." To Leclaire as to Godin, the sharing of
profits was an act of justice and good business.
Godin stressed the former in his message to the
world, and Leclaire the latter in argument with his
men and outside critics. " The guarantees of
existence," said Godin [1] " derive from the natural
right of everyone to the produce of Nature and
Society. The organizations of these other guarantees
presupposes the participation of the worker in
profits, or rather, the association of labour and
capital." " According to the critics," argued
Leclaire in 1870, " my staff, my men, and myself,
are a tribe of *partageux*." [*Partageur* means a sharer,
and *partageux* a communist.] " I beg their pardon,
the sentiment of property is too strong among us
for this to be so. The share of profit which our
co-workers enjoy is a legitimate gain, the fruit of
their labour. . . ." " I saw," he stated on an earlier
occasion, " that it paid me better to make more
and to give an interest in the profits to my workers
who helped me, than to make less and give them no
such interest."

When Leclaire was a young man, the law of
succession and the structure of business in France
was such that on the owner's death it was frequent

[1] "Le Gouvernement," p. 456.

for a concern to be valued and sold, good-will
included. "The buyer of the clientèle," exclaims
Leclaire, "keeps the good workers and officials
whose looks do not announce old age. But those
whose appearance discovers the least failing in
strength are mercilessly discharged." This he
thought a cruel injustice. In 1848, when he was
an unsuccessful candidate for the National Assembly
of the second Republic and again in 1865 as Mayor
of Herblay, he advocated municipal labour exchanges
of the sort which have since come to be. But this
did not suffice for him in his own concern. He set
out to perpetuate it, not as a modern joint stock
company is perpetuated by the random transfer
of shares through inheritance or sale, but by the
endowment of his workers with a corporate existence.
To-day, Leclaire's successors have only a limited
life interest in the business. In the event of its
being broken up for any reason whatsoever the title
to property, reserve, and good-will is legally vested
in the so-called Mutual Aid Society, composed
exclusively of the workers.

What immediately prompted Leclaire to the
establishment of the Mutual Aid Society in 1838
was the terrible sickness among painters due to
lead poisoning. Finding on examination that out
of the sixty-three members on its sick list 30 per cent.
had lead colic, he resolved to look for a cure. He

made himself a chemist, studied, experimented, and discovered that oxide of zinc was a harmless yet adequate substitute for white lead. Thereupon he leased a zinc mine and produced his own zinc. In 1878, when Charles Robert, President of the Mutual Aid Society, wrote his brilliant monograph on Leclaire, " the use of white zinc compared with that of white lead in painting operations is indicated by a percentage figure of about 75."[1]

Copartnership, for the sake of peace, or to use Nasmyth's metaphor, for the sake of suppressing the volcano, would have seemed to Leclaire a contemptible vanity. He desired that his work should endure, and to this end fought a battle with his men in 1860. When the members of the Mutual Aid Society were requested by him in that year to renounce their right to the eventual partition of its funds, many showed themselves unwilling. Thereupon Leclaire threatened, as he had legally the power, to swamp the Society with batches of new members who would each one of them come in for a share of the spoil. The threat sufficed. The Society was made permanent, and became the foundation on which the edifice of Copartnership was built. In 1863, the Society was made a partner in the business. In 1869 the terms of partnership were broadened and consolidated by the document

[1] Robert's "Leclaire," p. 41.

fittingly called a Charter of Labour. "*Ermite à Herblay*" was the new style on Leclaire's card—for thither he had retired in 1865 to "efface himself." "*Maison Leclaire, devenue Valmé Brugniot et Cie,*" is the style of the house to-day.

The firm's capital, which in 1869 was £12,000, has since been increased to £32,000. Leclaire took out what he put in, £4000, asking nothing on account of improved value.[1] At present the two managing partners own £12,000 of the capital and the Mutual Aid Society £20,000, and on the whole of this a fixed interest of 5 per cent. is paid. The liability of the managing partners is unlimited, that of the Society is limited. Leclaire gave much thought to the methods by which future managers should be appointed, as well as to their powers in regard to the rest of the establishment. In the statutes of 1869, he provided that the share of a retiring manager should be paid out to him in proportion as that of his successor was paid in, and that the latter's share should be met by the reservation of two-thirds of his part in the profits until the whole was discharged. Thus he made it possible for any worker in the establishment, who had the necessary brains without the necessary fortune, to succeed to the highest office. The managers are elected for life by a chosen

[1] Leclaire died worth about £50,000, a sum comparatively small for a long career of business success.

body of the workers in General Assembly. Once elected they have all the powers necessary for direction. As Leclaire said to his men as far back as 1840, " I think no one will imagine that on the day when the association is established, everybody will be free to do as he pleases. No ! gentlemen, it can never at any time be thus. . . . I am the master in my business."

The workers, however, have two effective channels for the exertion of influence in the firm's policy : collectively, through their Mutual Aid Society, which owns five-eighths of the capital, and individually through membership in the *Noyau* or Nucleus. At its original formation the members of the Nucleus were selected by Leclaire from the ranks of the previously established Mutual Aid Society. To-day it is from the sum of the skilled permanent workers and officials that new members are co-opted by the Nucleus. The statutes enact that merit and not seniority is to be the chief consideration. The workers in the Nucleus are paid 2½d. per hour above the tariff rates of the city of Paris, they can claim of right to belong to the Mutual Aid Society, and they may receive permission to leave the house on temporary work without forfeiting their posts. When they meet in General Assembly once a year, they elect two delegates from their own number to examine the firm's books, and see that the profits are fixed and

E

shared in accordance with the statutes. They also
appoint foremen for the different shops to hold
office for one year at a time. No one may be expelled
from the Nucleus except on the decision of the
Conciliation Committee, which consists of the
managing partners, five workers or foremen, and
three members of the office staff. If occasion should
arise, as, for example, the necessity of electing a
new managing director, a General Assembly of the
Nucleus is summoned extraordinarily.

In 1877, out of 763 workers, temporary and
permanent, 117 workers were members of the
Nucleus, 104 were eligible, but not yet elected.
For 1910-11 the following figures are available :—
Office staff, 61 ; workmen, members of the Nucleus,
136 ; *auxiliaires*, 1004 ; apprentices, 36.

The Nucleus is thus one of the corner stones. The
Mutual Aid Society is the other. The funds of this
are derived from the 5 per cent. interest on its capital
(it holds five-eighths of the whole), from its share in
the surplus profits (now five-sixteenths of the total),
from an entrance fee of 16s. per member, and lastly,
from fines and *pourboires*. " Requests for gratuities,"
says Article XXVI of the rules, " are humiliating to
those who make them and offensive to those from
whom they are asked." But a gratuity voluntarily
given may be accepted and must be handed over
to the Society. The Society gives benefits of two

kinds [1] : (1) medical benefit and sick pay, unless the illness be due to intoxication or brawling ; (2) retiring pensions of £15 to £60 per annum, with reversion at half-rates to widows and orphan children. All workers in the establishment, whether members of the Nucleus or not, are eligible for membership, candidates being rejected only on grounds of bad conduct or immorality. Article XV of the house provides that any workman *not* a member of the Society who, while working for the firm, is permanently injured, shall have the right to a retiring pension. The members of the Society in their General Assembly elect their president and an administrative Family Council of eighteen (*Conseil de Famille*) which meets every three months and has a standing committee of twelve for the inspection of sick cases. The president, who is the Society's official representative as a partner in the firm, was at the beginning Leclaire himself. Since then he has been by rule chosen from outside. M. Charles Robert in this way succeeded Leclaire in the presidency, and has in turn been succeeded by M. Leopold Mabilleau. Although by French law a partner with limited liability, such as this Society is, does not take part in the practical direction of the business, nevertheless it has certain rights of inspection, and these the president exercises on its behalf.

[1] A. Trombert, " La Participation aux bénéfices," p. 189, Paris, 1912.

Finally—for this is the conclusion up to which the preceding matter naturally leads—Article XVIII of the statutes enacts that after the payment of 5 per cent. interest on all capital the remaining profits shall be distributed as follows :—

$\frac{3}{16}$ to the two managing partners.
$\frac{5}{16}$ to the Mutual Aid Society.
$\frac{8}{16}$ (in cash) to the workers and members of the office staff.

At first only the members of the Nucleus received a share in the profits, but by Article XVII of the rules of 1869, " All workers, whatever their position, as well as all officials and apprentices working for the house, shall receive a share in the profits." Each man's share is determined as follows : Suppose the divisible $\frac{8}{16}$ (or 50 per cent.) of profit is £1000 and the total of wages and salaries is £10,000, then each £1 of wage or salary gets £$\frac{1,000}{10,000}$, *i.e.* 2s. If a man's wages for the year amount to £100 (extras are excluded), then his share is 2s. × 100, *i.e.* £10.

Many of the rules in the Maison Leclaire recall the statutes of the Familistère at Guise. Especially does the Nucleus resemble the 1st class members (*Associés*). Leclaire, like Godin, endeavoured to lodge the chief power in an aristocracy of picked workers into whose ranks there should be a constant stream of new admissions. Inasmuch as all the workers, whether members of this aristocracy or not, share in the profits, the aristocracy should have no inducement to degenerate into a close corporation. Political democracy, thought these two great Frenchmen, is a noble and a right thing, but industrial democracy needs to be protected against itself. For while political mistakes lead to failure and more taxes, industrial mistakes lead to failure and extinction.

Congeners in England and France

The achievements of Godin have deservedly won a prominent place in the records of the Labour Copartnership Association in England. M. Prudhommeaux's book, "Twenty years of Copartnership at Guise," has been translated into English by Mr Aneurin Williams. Several of the workers' productive societies in this country have adopted Godin's scheme of repartition, for example, the Walsall Locks and Cart-Gear Society which, after a fixed payment to capital, divides the remainder between wages of labour and the interest of capital. " This principle of division," said Earl Grey in his Mansion House address of May 9, 1912, " has always seemed to me to be absolutely fair and to be capable of being easily applied to many industries." True, no doubt, but it is not so easy to find the will and

the brains to create the organisation in which this
scheme of division may operate, and these are the
important things. As Godin said, " If those who
know not knew, and if those who could would,
social difficulties would be soon solved."

A foreign student might be surprised to find that
the Labour Copartnership Association, the official
spokesman of the workers' productive societies
and of the businesses practising Copartnership, is
also closely associated with one of the most recent
phases of co-operative activity, the Tenants' Copartnership Societies.[1] For structurally these are
without doubt associations of consumers. They
provide house-room for their members, even as the
store provides food and clothing, and although they
may find it possible to associate the building
operatives on the estates in a share of their profits,
yet this is obviously but a minor incident in their
purpose. These societies take an area of ground,
which they develop as an estate with buildings
and the necessary places for recreation.   The tenants
do not buy their houses, but rent them from the
society whose share capital they hold : surplus
profit, after payment of 5 per cent. on capital, going
to the tenants in proportion to their rental.   This
solves in a manner the problem of the unearned
increment, for any gain does not go to the share-

[1] Report on Co-operative Societies, 1912, pp. li-liv.

holders as such or to the individual tenants in the improving locality, but by swelling the surplus profits it necessarily benefits all the tenants of the society as tenants, in the shape of increased dividends on their rental. Sixteen such societies with a membership of 2511 and a cost value of land and buildings owned amounting to £638,284 are recorded for 1909 : and a pamphlet issued by the Copartnership Tenants, Limited, the federal head of the movement, states that this figure of £638,284 had reached £1,190,000 in December 1912.[1]

Godin was very contemptuous of houses for working men, little shanties without influence on the manners and well-being of the population, the evidence of unregulated and cramping individualism. In contrast with these his *Palais Social*, in which rich and poor lived together, would be an organisation economically cheaper and socially more conducive to corporate well-being. Most Englishmen have a feeling that Godin here was wrong. The social palace suggests the confinement and publicity of a barracks, and experience seems to show that living in common, whether in the college of a university or in an urban settlement, costs more than private living of an equivalent standard. But there was one clear benefit and one most subtle truth in the *Palais social*, as Godin conceived

[1] "The Growth of an Idea," p. 12.

for society and realised it in the Familistère. The benefit is none other than the benefit which is afforded by the Tenants' Copartnership Societies. " To take from it," said Godin,[1] " all character of speculation, it would be well to organise it in such a way that the return to capital should be limited to a maximum of 4 per cent. or 5 per cent. for example, and that the profits above this yielded by the apartments should be shared among the tenants in proportion to the amount of their rents. This sharing of the rental revenue is calculated to attach the population to the success of the enterprise and to encourage them in sound economies." The subtle truth is this. Over against the Familistère stands the Foundry ; and as far as possible the workers in the Foundry, masters and men, rich and poor, live in the Familistère. The branding of certain districts as " working-class " and of others as " well-to-do " is one of the most repulsive as it is one of the most dangerous features of modern society. And yet, if we are frank, we who are of the middle or upper class, must avow our objection to living amid a crowd of strangers whose habits may be less gentle than our own. It would involve a mutual discomfort. But no decent landlord in the country finds it anything less than a pride to live among his tenants and labourers ; and would any

[1] " Le Gouvernement," p. 535.

decent works-manager object to living near his men, would any decent man be embarrassed by the neighbourhood of his foreman or manager ? No. Godin said no, and proved it. We shake our heads sighing feebly for the good old days when the apprentice supped at his master's board and finally married his master's daughter. Meanwhile, the West End stands separate from the East, condescending at times to charitable raids across the barriers of the City, which has no time for politics, or past the quiet purlieus of Whitehall, which welcomes anything that may facilitate the accumulation of statistics.

A main product of our modern social democracy is the organisation of effort from the standpoint of the consumer. While it is just possible to argue that in the case of the municipality economic enterprise has been forced on it by the pressure of the vote, this contention is inadmissible against the vast federation of the co-operative stores and against the new societies of Copartnership tenants. But as surely as municipal trading and large scale production by the co-operative stores are destined to increase, so surely will they find the problem of capital and labour fastening itself on them with its old dilemma. It is well for the Copartnership estates that they have started life under the guidance of men who are favourable to Copartnership with labour, and who are not strangers to the monumental creation of Godin at Guise.

Leclaire's lesson is less pretentious, but very direct. Profit-sharing as an isolated device is unsubstantial: profit-sharing as a kernel of Copartnership is a just and wise thing. Now Copartnership may be of a simple or advanced kind. It is of a simple kind when the sharing of profits is associated with their employment in some permanent form, in a sickness or pension or savings fund, or in a regulated plan of investment in the firm's capital. In all these cases the workers are in no sense the directors of the firm's policy, and it is not contemplated that they should secure a controlling interest in the share capital. But in the management of the funds or in the plan of investment the workers will naturally have a voice and status. Co-partnership is of an advanced kind when the position of the workers in the business is so deeply rooted that the abandonment of copartnership would necessitate a perceptible change in the composition of the directorate or a serious change in the composition of the capital. Between the two kinds of Copartnership there is no hard and fast line. Advanced Copartnership when attained at all is likely to emerge from a previous experience of Copartnership of a simpler order. This natural sequence is observable in the history of the Maison Leclaire.

The lean Report on Profit-sharing and Labour Copartnership in the United Kingdom issued from the Board of Trade at the end of 1912 [1] contains a class headed, " Conversion of ordinary businesses into Co-operative Societies." Herein are noted three experiments, one which liquidated in 1897, a second which was worked on a profit-sharing basis from 1897 to 1901 and as a co-operative society from 1902 till its collapse in 1910, and a third, the very different and very successful concern of William Thomson & Sons, Ltd., of Huddersfield. With regard to the second, the Haslemere Builders, Ltd., the Report states that the founder, Mr H., "found the results of the profit-sharing arrangements ' most discouraging.' He attributed the unsuccessful financial results of the business to the want of energy and carefulness displayed by his workmen generally (especially on distant jobs) ; on the other hand the profit-sharing scheme made many of his men ' extremely loyal.' At the end of 1900, Mr H. ' abandoned profit-sharing,' in order to introduce other arrangements. . . ." This is enough. To abandon profit-sharing at a critical juncture and substitute Copartnership for it is like taking off one's vest in mid-winter in order to make room for the coat. In sections of its rules which have nothing

[1] [Cd. 6496.] An earlier and fuller report was issued in 1894 [C. 7458].

whatever to do with profit-sharing, the Maison Leclaire makes careful provision for the good conduct and economy of its workers on country jobs. Profit-sharing or no profit-sharing, it is the manager's business to elicit energy and carefulness from his men. When by his personality and method he is in the way of securing this, then first can he give to his results a concrete permanence by the gradual introduction of Copartnership.

This is what has been done at Huddersfield. In 1886 Mr George Thomson,[1] the owner of an old established worsted manufactory trading as William Thomson & Sons, converted his business into a Society registered under the Industrial and Provident Society's Act. The present constitution of the Society is as follows : Out of a share capital of £13,027, some £4000 is held by co-operative societies, mainly retail stores, £3313 is held by employees of the Society and the remainder by various individuals. The major part of the loan capital, to wit, £13,190, is held by Mr Thomson himself, and of the remainder £2000 is in the hands of various Trade Union organisations. The rules of the Society provide that after the payment of 5 per cent. on loan and share capital the surplus profit shall be divided into two equal parts, one half going to the workers in proportion to their wages,

[1] *Cf.* the account given in the Board of Trade Report, 1912, pp. 87-90.

and the other half to purchasers in proportion to their custom. The purchasers' dividend, however, is only paid to the two co-operative wholesale societies, general traders preferring the usual terms of credit. The workers' half is paid not in cash, but in shares or payments on account of shares in the Society. Mr Thomson is managing director for life, subject to removal by the vote of the Society, and as manager he is empowered to "control all businesses carried on by the Society and engage, remove, or discharge all assistant managers, salesmen, or employees of every description required to conduct such business, and fix their duties, salaries, or other remuneration at such rates, and require them to give security in any form approved by the Committee, as he may determine, subject to the duty of regularly reporting all such acts to the Committee." Furthermore, he may nominate his successor subject to confirmation by the special general meeting. Many years ago in 1891, Mr Thomson's proposal that he should surrender a part of the full managing authority reserved to him was unanimously declined. The committee, whose functions are mainly consultative, consists of the manager, two employees of the Society, three representatives of share-holding co-operative societies, one representative of the Huddersfield Trades Council, and the secretary of the Weavers'

Association. If the committee thinks fit, it may devote a portion of the profits (prior to the surplus distribution) to an Assurance and Pension Fund : in which case the amount so devoted is regulated by a sliding scale, varying according to the wages bill and total of net profits, but not exceeding 5 per cent. of the wages paid during the year. The Society's sales, which were at the outset about £22,500 a year, were £46,392 in 1911, the custom withdrawn by traders hostile to the co-operative connection having been successfully replaced by that of the co-operative stores themselves. After the payment of the 5 per cent. interest on capital, the employees clear share in profits has been equivalent on the average to 3·3 per cent. on wages. Figures for 1912 :—

Profit after deduction of 5 per cent. interest £4148
Allotted to Workers 870
Allotted to Pension Fund.   .   .   . 1075

The Society works a forty-eight hours' week, and in December 1911, in commemoration of its twenty-fifth anniversary, it announced an all-round increase of wage and raising of the minimum pension rates. As evidence of the spirit which animates the Society it may be mentioned, first, that on several occasions when the 5 per cent. interest could not be met from profits, the workpeople have voluntarily made good the deficiency, contributing in this way £2224 in all (which has been repaid to them in cash out of the profits of 1912), and furthermore that in 1890 one of the workmen who had invented a great improvement in weaving, instead of patenting it for his own benefit, presented his invention to the Society ! Our business, says Mr Thomson, is founded on the following :—" No religion that ever was preached on this earth of God's rounding ever proclaimed any salvation to makers of bad goods, . . . all political economy, as well as all higher virtue, depends first on sound work."

The old established firm of J. T. and J. Taylor, Ltd.,[1] woollen manufacturers of Batley, has steadily progressed towards the advanced type of Copartnership. In 1892 the present owner, Mr T. C. Taylor, M.P. (still the largest shareholder), acquired the full control of the business, and then began profit-sharing with managers and foremen. In 1896 the principle was extended to the rank and file, dating back to the beginning of 1895, and the business was converted into a private limited company, with a view to sharing profits in the form of dividend-producing shares given out of the profits. More than half the

[1] Owing to a misunderstanding, not mentioned by *name* in the Board of Trade Report, 1912. But *cf.* Annual Reports of Labour Copartnership Association, especially 24th in 1908-9, p. 12.

capital of the company is now (1913) owned by the
workers, numbering 1624, of whom half are females.
Under the arrangements in force since 1908, surplus
profit over 5 per cent. is divided at the same percentage rate between capital and wages ; and each
employee must allow his portion of profits to accumulate in shares until it reaches a sum equal to
his year's earnings.   Of any amount above that he
has free disposal.   Employees over twenty-one and
with not less than five years' service, who hold
shares equal to half a year's wages, get double bonus.
Employees with less than a year's service get no
bonus, the fractions due in respect of these being
devoted to the Workers' Benefit Fund.   The shares
of the company are divided into A Owner's and B
Bonus Shares.   The bonus shares confer no voting
power.   In the judgment of Mr Taylor and his fellow-
managers such powers might endanger the success
of the business, which is of so complex a character
as to require expert knowledge and decision to an
exceptional degree.   Employees are not allowed now
to sell their shares to one another, unless they are
leaving the business.   If they go into other employment, they must sell them at par to the owners or
other workers ; but the widows of workers and
retired workers themselves, the "old boys" of the
business, are allowed to retain them as long as is
practicable.   For, by the Company's Act of 1907, a

private company which does not publish balance-sheets may not have more than fifty shareholders, who are not workers in the firm. Since 1895 the workers have received in shares and dividend on them, and in amounts passed to the Workers' Benefit Fund, considerably over £100,000. The dividend on shares during the years 1910-12 has averaged 13⅓ per cent., and the bonus on wages (given in the shape of shares) 8⅓ or 16⅔ per cent., according to qualifications. The dividends for the whole period have been a little over 11 per cent. on capital and over 7 per cent. on wages.

It is stated that no firm in the trade pays better wages. But what about losses and depression ? " I can speak," says Mr Taylor,[1] " from experience. In 1897 and 1898 we had no dividends, and I have yet to hear the first word of reproach or mistrust from any one of my copartners." " Our business ought to be a true Friendly Society "; and, faithfully to this ideal, the financial arrangements are only one part of the many-sided contact between employer and employed. For in common with a number of firms, this firm anticipated the sickness, sanatoria, and other benefits, which are now generalised by law. The value of this legislation will in no small measure depend on its success in supplementing without destroying these voluntary instalments of it.

[1] *Contemporary Review*, May 1912.

F

We may conclude our account of copartnership in its advanced form with two further samples from France.

The paper-making establishment of Laroche, Joubert & Co., Angoulême,[1] registered as a co-operative society, began profit-sharing in 1882. The profits are distributed in cash, 25 per cent. to capital, 25 per cent. to the manager and managing council, and 50 per cent. to the workers, whose share is regulated by the two factors of earnings and seniority taken in combination. There are no mutual aid funds within the body of the establishment, all its members being said to belong to societies having these purposes in the districts where they reside. Of £150,000 of capital, nearly one-third is held by the workers of the different grades, either present or past members of the firm. A co-operative council with advisory functions assists the management. It meets several times a year and comprises representatives of the office-staff and ordinary workers. Luzzatti, the distinguished Italian economist and statesman, made a strict inquiry into the condition of the society in 1898 and pronounced most favourably upon it. For sixty years there had been no suggestion of a strike, and the prosperity of the business had grown steadily. In 1909 the society employed from 1100 to 1200 workers.

[1] A. Trombert, "La Participation aux bénéfices," p. 195.

The shopping establishment of the *Bon Marché*[1] of Paris, a huge concern with a trade of £9,000,000 per annum, has developed Copartnership on lines more characteristically French. In 1880 Mme. Boucicaut, widow of M. Aristide Boucicaut, the founder of the business, associated some of the head assistants in the business ; to-day the whole capital £1,800,000 is held by present and retired members of the establishment. The shareholders in 1900 numbered 760, and these alone share directly in the profits. But all workers of five years' service and upwards, who are outside the upper circle of shareholders, share in the benefits of the several provident institutions financed by the establishment. The chief of these is the *Prévoyance Boucicaut*, which on its installation in 1876 had 128 members, and in July 1911, 3346. The sums paid into the fund are credited to individual account on the basis of earnings, and after a certain period of service they become the disposable property of the recipients. Female members who marry are entitled to realise their accounts, whatever length of service they may have reached, and even if they leave the house. This is supplemented by a pension fund endowed by Mme. Boucicaut in 1886, a further pension and sickness fund established in 1892, and a special fund for assisting the widows and orphans of deceased

[1] A. Trombert, "La Participation aux bénéfices," p. 209.

workers. Female employees whose families do not live in Paris are boarded in the house ; and the whole staff is supplied with a free meal every morning. In July 1911, the *Bon Marché* had :—

916	Servants with a period of service of			20	years and upwards.
135	,,	,,	,,	19	,,
147	,,	,,	,,	18	,,
114	,,	,,	,,	17	,,
121	,,	,,	,,	16	,,
108	,,	,,	,,	15	,,
103	,,	,,	,,	14	,,

(1644

Stability of service is the natural outcome of stable organisation. A shopping establishment is a form of business which lends itself to such an organisation. But no other great shop-keepers appear to have emulated the example of M. and Mme. Boucicaut Godin and Leclaire died childless. M. and Mme. Boucicaut lost their only child. Having no natural successors, these employers adopted their workpeople. What is unnatural to the normal man is natural to those whose genius is attuned to that higher law of Nature, which the noblest minds have ever striven to decipher and express.

CHAPTER III

SINCE 1909 there has been in operation in the firm
of Lever Bros., Ltd., soap manufacturers, of Port
Sunlight, Cheshire, and since 1911, in its associated
companies at home and abroad, a scheme [1] which,
in the phrase of its author, has for its object, not
profit-sharing, but Copartnership in prosperity.
It depends for its legal validity upon a trust deed
entitled "The Copartnership Trust in Lever Bros.,
Ltd.," and its main features are as follows : Partnership certificates are issued to all servants of the firm
from the directors downwards who, being over
twenty-five years of age, and having served the
firm for not less than five years, have qualified themselves to receive these certificates by compliance
with the terms of the Copartnership agreement,
The signatories to this, without committing themselves to any sort of pecuniary liability, promise
that they "will not waste time, labour, materials,
or money in the discharge of their duties, but will
loyally and faithfully further the interests of the

[1] See speech of Sir W. H. Lever, Feb. 25, 1909, printed as supple-
ment to *Progress*, April, 1909 (a monthly magazine of the employees
of Lever Bros.).

company." Entry into the scheme is optional.
The allocation of the certificates is left to the discretion of the trustees, who are the directors, and in
this work they are assisted by an advisory committee
of twelve, representing and elected by the separate
grades of employees.* Any copartner who is dis-
satisfied with the decision of the trustees has the
right of appeal to the majority shareholder (Sir W.
H. Lever). Once issued the partnership certificates
confer a right to dividend, the nature of which is
specified in the Trust Deed. After payment of prior
charges and of 5 per cent. on the ordinary shares, the
surplus of the moneys declared by the company to be
disposable for dividend is divided *pari passu* at the
same rate per cent. between the holders of the
ordinary shares and the holders of partnership
certificates. By the end of 1911 £275,429 of these
certificates had been issued, and the ordinary
dividend being 15 per cent., the certificates con-
sequently drew 10 per cent., which amounted to
£27,542. The dividends are paid to an employees'
savings bank account opened for the copartners
individually, and they may be spent, saved, or
invested as the latter please. When a copartner
reaches the age of retirement, or before that date
is retired by the company through no fault of his
own, the partnership certificates are exchanged for
preferential certificates yielding 5 per cent. interest,

and ranking for dividend after the 5 per cent. paid on
the ordinary shares of the company. The preferential
certificates lapse on the holder's death, but are continued for the widow unless and until she remarries.

The nature of the partnership certificates and the
position of the majority shareholder in regard to
them are peculiar. They do not in themselves
represent money, and they are of no more value
than waste paper until a profit over and above
5 per cent. on the ordinary capital has been earned.
If the holder voluntarily leaves the business before
the appointed age of retirement, and not owing to
permanent incapacity caused by ill-health, or if
the holder in the opinion of the trustees, subject
to an appeal to the majority shareholder, is guilty
of a breach of his agreement to render loyal service,
then the certificates are cancelled and the rights
attaching to them are absolutely extinguished.
Thus, neither these partnership certificates, nor the
preferential certificates into which they may be
ultimately converted, are permanently-owned
property, but merely paper of a nominal capital
value regulating the distribution of certain sums
to their temporary holders. However, these sums,
the dividends on the certificates, are the legal and
untied property of the recipients. Furthermore,
the majority shareholder decides for himself how
large the annual issue of certificates shall be. In

his own words, " I can give more, I can give less, I can give none." The Trust Deed merely specifies an aggregate limit of £500,000 ·which cannot be passed without his consent. In practice the scale of issue has been, and for some further time is intended to be, 10 per cent. on the salaries and wages actually earned. Therefore, with the present dividend of 10 per cent. the employee is credited in his savings account with 10 per cent. on 10 per cent., *i.e.*, 1 per cent. on his wages for the current year together with 10 per cent. on the accumulated partnership scrip similarly issued in previous years. There is a maximum of £200 nominal value which any worker earning less than £100 a year may thus accumulate in certificates, and therefore (on a dividend of 10 per cent.) a maximum of £20 which can be paid per annum to his savings account. There are corresponding maxima at higher figures for the higher paid workers and officials. It may - be mentioned that the first issue of certificates in 1909 was made retrospective to 1901, so that an issue on the basis of eight, seven, or a lesser number of years was made straight away to those possessing the necessary qualifications.

The scheme is new and must await the test of time, but the possibility that it may find imitators will justify some general comments.

To begin with, the business in which it has been introduced is an exceptionally successful one, and the person mainly responsible for this success is still the majority shareholder. Sir W. H. Lever argues that capital, like wages, has a right, in the first instance, to a limited remuneration, which he has fixed at 5 per cent., having regard to the rate which the investor who does not actively employ his own capital may reasonably hope to earn. But many old-established companies, as well as many new ones in their early days, earn only 5 per cent., or less, on their ordinary shares. In such concerns copartnership on this basis and with this justification is impracticable. But when a business built up by a few individuals is later converted into a public concern, the rate of interest declared on the shares depends considerably upon the terms of conversion. If such a scheme of copartnership were successfully introduced and consolidated in the private stage, and if at the time of conversion regard were had to the necessity for its maintenance, then it might continue to flourish as part of a normal joint-stock structure in which the remuneration of business talent is secured among the expenses of production and most of the risks are run by shareholders with no greater tie of interest than an appetite for dividends.

Would-be imitators must also have regard **to**

the nature of the soap-making industry. For in
modern industry an employee may be specialised
in two ways : first, with reference to the skill
required in a particular grade of his industry, and
secondly, with reference to the practices of the firm
by whom he is employed. Specialisation of the
latter order is likely to be important in industries
occupied by firms which make, and possibly have
been pioneers in making, articles of a proprietary
order, of which Sunlight Soap is a notable example.
In such industries employers will gain by having
round them for a long period of years workers who
know their special ways and have an inkling of their
secrets. Conversely, loss of service in a particular
firm may mean to the worker a serious diminution
in his market value. In such businesses, therefore,
the permanent ties which this kind of Copartnership
involves are particularly likely to be of mutual
benefit.

Finally, the good faith of the scheme has been
warranted by previous experience of the firm's
generosity. Coming as an additional endowment
in a long series of benefits—model housing, benefit
fund, holiday fund, &c.—it was accepted by employees without fear of its being a covert attempt
to reduce wages or fetter the wage-earners. Unlike
so many profit-sharing schemes, we find it blessed
by the secretary of the local trade union, who

declared in 1909 :   " After paying trade union wages
to all his staff, after giving concessions in the way
of a forty-eight hours' week, . . . this scheme is
a thing to be proud of, and Mr Lever deserves the
congratulations and the thanks of every trade
unionist in the district." [1]

But in less favourable circumstances the merits
of the scheme would be its defects. By the device
of partnership certificates the employees are given
immediately the sense of co-ownership, and the
subsequent reinvestment of the accruing dividends
in the real stock of the company is altogether
voluntary.   In other schemes, where a bonus is paid
on wages and part is reserved for investment in
the company's stock, the worker saves under com-
pulsion, and only draws substantial interest on a
capital holding at a later stage of the process.
There is a convenience, too, in the fact that the
Trust Deed, while suggesting fixity of operation,
does not regulate the issue of the certificates themselves, but merely the rate of dividend they shall
carry in case surplus profits are made. In a bad
trade year, when there was no surplus to divide,
the certificates could still be issued, although these
and those outstanding would receive no dividend
for the year in question. In this way the gap

[1] Mr Nelson at the first distribution of partnership certificates.
July 23, 1909.

between good and bad years would be fortunately
bridged without pressure on the company to weaken
its commercial position by excessive distribution.
If we add to this the fact that a worker forfeits his
certificates by striking or by passing to other employment, the strong position of the employer is clearly
seen. In ungenerous or imprudent hands this
scheme might result in large issues of scrip carrying
no market value or legal status, and imposing on
the issuers no obligation beyond that of sharing a
surplus profit which might be artificially lessened
by rearrangements of capitalisation. And in the
meantime the workers' hands would have been tied
because revolt would entail the forfeiture of the scrip
and of the future benefits expected from it. It is,
perhaps, needless to say that these possibilities are
in no wise suggested by the policy of the firm with
which this scheme has originated. In Liverpool and
district Port Sunlight stands out as a model place
of good employment.

The model for the second type of Copartnership,
which has now the merit of long approved success,
is provided by the South Metropolitan Gas Company.
The history of Copartnership in the gas industry
divides itself into two periods. The eighteen years
from 1889 to 1907 were a time of experiment, during
which the late Sir George Livesey, as chairman of the

South Metropolitan and director of the neighbouring South Suburban Gas Company, was pioneering the new system and elaborating its details. By the beginning of 1907, *i.e.*, eighteen years after its inception in the South Metropolitan, copartnership was confined to five companies—three in London and two in the provinces. Then followed a rapid extension, the impetus to which was given by two addresses of Sir George Livesey at meetings attended by gas engineers and managers in November 1907,[1] and June 1908.[2] Each address was followed by keen and critical discussion, as the result of which a considerable body of expert opinion in the gas industry seems to have been converted to the idea. Of the thirty-six gas companies which are quoted by the Labour Copartnership Association[3] as practising some form of copartnership and profit sharing, practically all have schemes which are based on the models drawn up by Sir George Livesey.

The financial side of the South Metropolitan scheme is based on a sliding scale which applies both to the shareholders' dividend and the copartners' bonus. At 3s. 1d. the standard price of gas per

[1] Sir Geo. Livesey : "Employers and Employed and Copartnership," a paper read before the Southern District Association of Gas Engineers and Managers, Nov. 14, 1907.

[2] Sir Geo. Livesey : "Copartnership," a paper read before the Institution of Gas Engineers, June 16, 1908.

[3] 26th Report, 1911, p. 11.

1000 cubic feet, the shareholders' dividend is limited by law to 4 per cent. and the copartners' bonus is *nil*. For each 1d. reduction in the price of gas the shareholders get a further sum of 2s. 8d. per cent. in dividend and the copartners $\frac{3}{4}$ per cent. on their wages. That is to say, the bonus instead of varying directly with profits varies with the factor which governs profits, and rises as the price of gas falls. The price being in 1912 2s. 2d., or eleven units below 3s. 1d., the shareholders received per £100 of stock £4+£1, 9s. 4d. (£5, 9s. 4d. in all), and the co-partners a bonus of $\frac{3}{4} \times 11$, or 8$\frac{1}{4}$ per cent. Salaried officials and office staff as well as manual workers are eligible for the scheme, and, in point of fact, all the company's servants are copartners —although it may be necessary temporarily to exclude a worker who has violated the terms of the agreement. It is to the interest, therefore, of the employees, as well as of the shareholders, that gas should be sold at the lowest practicable price ; and the interest of these two parties is thereby reconciled with the interests of the third party, the consumer.

The bonus, which is paid once a year, is calculated on the weekly wage, no account being taken of overtime and no deduction being made for absence through sickness up to eight weeks per annum. The bonus, however, is not paid out in cash—it is credited to the copartner by entry in his pass-book under two heads, one half being carried to trust account for investment in the company's ordinary stock, and the other half being retained on savings account at 3 per cent. interest, withdrawable only under special circumstances. Copartners are forbidden to sell or pledge their stock, and a breach of this rule results in expulsion from the scheme. But the past bonuses can in no circumstances be forfeited, the savings and stock are the individual and absolute property of the copartner. If he leaves the company or is discharged he has the choice of retaining his stock or of taking with him the full cash equivalent.

Variability of bonus, compulsory saving, and part investment in the company's stock characterise also the copartnership schemes of the other companies. Companies with fixed maximum dividends have to arrive at their standard price differently. Thus, in the Liverpool United Gas Light Company, the latest big adherent to Copartnership, this price has been fixed at 2s. 8d., the price of gas in 1902, and the price of gas being 2s. 1d. in 1911, the scheme was then launched with the respectable bonus of $\frac{3}{4} \times 7$, or $5\frac{1}{4}$ per cent. In some schemes all the bonus up to a certain sum, say £20, is reserved for investment ; in others the withdrawable half is freely withdrawable. The South Metropolitan has been so pro-

minently the pioneer company that the merits of Copartnership in the gas industry may be best appraised
by reference to the experience of this company.
The financial advantages to the employees are
evident.   In most of the copartnership gas companies the bonus is in the neighbourhood of 5 per
cent. on wages.   In the South Metropolitan,[1] where
the present rate is 8¼ per cent., over half a million
has been paid in bonus since 1889, and the employees
now hold over £300,000 of the company's ordinary
stock.   Has the bonus been at the expense of wages ?

[1] With reference to the hours worked in the South Metropolitan
Gas Company, the following statement may be made on the authority
of the present chairman, Dr Charles Carpenter.   In the early part
of 1889, the Retort House men asked for and obtained an 8-hour
day.   In the following mid-winter they struck against Copartnership (or, as it was then called, profit-sharing) which was offered
voluntarily to all men in the Company's employ for acceptance by
those who would.   When the strike was over, it was put to the
men that they could please themselves whether they would work
on an 8-hour or a 12-hour day, the *pay being exactly proportional to
the work done in both cases.*   It was thus immaterial to the Company
which course they adopted.   The result of their choice was as follows
(the letters referring to the different works in the order of their
magnitude) :—

A. (largest Works)	.	.	.	. 12-hour shifts
B.	.	.	.	. 8 ,, ,,
C.	.	.	.	. 8 ,, ,,
D.	.	.	.	{ 8 ,, ,, in summer. { 12 ,, ,, in winter.
E.	.	.	.	. 12 ,, ,,
F. (smallest Works)	.	.	.	. 12 ,, ,,

This continued for many years, but as younger men came along

There are no figures or facts which would suggest this. Though there is no formal "union rate," the wages paid by the London companies practising Copartnership have been at least equal to those of other companies. The South Metropolitan Company gives its average for 1907 at 33s. per week ; and this figure, which includes a number of boys under twenty-one, does not include any of the salaried staff.

The attempt of the Gas-workers' Union to defeat the South Metropolitan scheme in 1889, and the threat that they would organise a further strike, of which no notice would be given, led to the insertion in the Copartnership agreement of a clause whereby the men bound themselves not to join the Union ; but many years ago the prohibition was withdrawn, and has never existed in the case of the other companies.

The retention of the bonus for deposit and stock prevents unthriftiness in the use of it. It cannot, like schemes of deferred benefits which are dependent on continuation in the service of the same company, restrict the employee's real freedom. On the con-

the adherents of the longer shifts became fewer and fewer, and for sometime past the Retort Houses have been wholly worked on 8-hour shifts. Since that time the 8-hour day has come into operation as the standard throughout all grades of employment, applying not only to carbonizing and "process" men, but to mechanics, artizans, and indeed all skilled and unskilled labour.

G

trary, the possession of property makes the man, as an individual, more independent. In one direction, clearly, his mobility is increased. Not infrequently cases have occurred where men have gone out to the Colonies, using their savings for the purchase of land.

It is not to be denied, however, that Copartnership introduces the worker in some degree to financial uncertainty and risk. Uncertainty attaches to the realisation of the bonus. The workers may respond to the scheme by extra zeal and devotion, but the bonus which is dependent on the price of gas may not advance correspondingly. It is, indeed, impossible to prove formally that the introduction of Copartnership has caused a progressive reduction in labour costs, and this in turn a progressive decrease in the price of gas. But Sir George Livesey contended before experts that the notable reduction in labour costs coincident with the progress of the scheme in the South Metropolitan and South Suburban Companies, although due in great measure to the introduction of labour-saving machinery, was in part due also to the greater efforts and economies made by the men. The saving in labour costs, he said, more than balanced the bonus paid out. " It is not true Copartnership if it does not benefit both employed and employer financially, for much of its success must be due to the employer, who not only initiates it, but on whom mainly depends its proper and successful working. It is, therefore, quite fair that he should benefit equally with his workmen, and my experience is that they are content it should be so." [1]

It is to be expected from the nature and position of the gas industry that increased efficiency of production will manifest itself in cheaper price. For, in the first place, the supply of gas is a distributive monopoly. Electric current, which the South Metropolitan Company does not supply, is, indeed, an increasingly formidable competitor; but, nevertheless, the gas industry is not exposed to such violent fluctuations of profitableness as, for example, are the jute and shipbuilding trades. In the second place, by the regulations already described, shareholders can only reap additional profits in proportion as prices are reduced. In the third place, the oscillations of demand are not acute.

It is not possible, however, to isolate one contributory cause in the cost of production and to say, " in this or that year the price of gas fell so much as the result of more efficient labour, which was itself the result of Copartnership." The facts as regards the South Metropolitan for the twenty-two years

[1] Livesey, " Employers and Employed and Copartnership," p. 19.

from 1889 to 1911 are these. From 1893, by which
date the scheme was firmly established, the price
fell 1d. a year down to 1900. In 1901, owing to a
big rise in the cost of raw materials, the price rose
7d. to 2s. 8d. In 1902 the price dropped again to
2s. 3d., and for the last two years it has been 2s. 2d.
Now it is to be noted that in the years from 1893
to 1900, when the scheme was on its trial, costs and
prices were falling in non-Copartnership as well
as in Copartnership concerns. The scheme was,
therefore, fortunate in its time of probation. If
the present rise in general prices extends appreciably
to the raw materials of the gas industry, it is probable
that the price of the products, gas itself, as well as
its highly important by-products, will rise, or, at
any rate, not decline further. Will this be fatal
to Copartnership, especially to those companies
which have but recently adopted it ? The experience of the South Metropolitan is that on two occasions, 1892 and 1901, sudden and serious reductions
of bonus were accepted without friction. The men
recognised, said Sir George Livesey, the perfect
fairness of consumers, shareholders, and employees
suffering together. They accepted as an essential
part of Copartnership the idea that the co-partners
—to the extent not of their wages but of their
bonus—should share in the risks of profit and loss
along with the other parties. However, it must be

recorded that in 1901, when the rise in price should have extinguished the bonus altogether, the company took advantage of the critical juncture to revise the bonus scale by bringing it into line with the scale applying to dividends, with the result that the bonus was only reduced from 9 per cent. to 3¾ per cent., instead of from 9 per cent. to *nil*. The lesson seems to be that the system will stand moderate fluctuations, and that a rise of price sufficient to extinguish the bonus can, if necessary, be met by a revision of the sliding scale.

The second element of risk to which the workers are introduced resides in the possible fluctuations of the stock in which their bonus is invested. Here, again, the position of the gas industry is favourable. Gas stocks in general are not the subject of great speculation. The recent downward fluctuations in the common and preferred shares of the United States Steel Corporation have militated against its scheme of privileged investment by employees, and a similar movement in the stocks of gas companies would undoubtedly inflict a strain on the plan of compulsory investment.

The general, as apart from the financial, merits of the scheme may now be examined. The Trade Unions, in London and Liverpool particularly, have opposed Copartnership on the ground that it strikes at the solidarity of labour. In one sense this allegation is true. Copartnership as an engine of social peace strikes, and is meant to strike, at a social ideal based on the war of classes with intervals of armed neutrality. In the first place, whilst a man is working under a Copartnership agreement, it is illegal for him to strike. For this agreement is also his contract of service running for a period of three or six or twelve months, and breach of contract by employees in gas and water undertakings renders them liable to criminal prosecution under the Conspiracy and Property Act of 1875, apart from possible procedure under the common law. This secures the company and its customers against a sudden strike by the workmen, and it also secures the workmen from external pressure to come out in sympathy. The agreement, however, binds the masters as well as the men, who, instead of being liable to the usual week's notice, are guaranteed continuous employment for a term of months.

Apart from this negative feature, the positive ties of Copartnership, culminating in the fact of part ownership, are calculated to discourage aggressive action which may damage the company's prosperity. But is not the workman thereby bartering his freedom for money and the things which money buys, bartering that freedom of organised action which our industrial democracy has struggled for a century to maintain ?   If the wage agreement and bonus provisions were the beginning and end of the scheme this risk would indeed be serious, but controlling these things or connected with them are certain institutions for collective action.

The management of the scheme rests with a Copartnership Committee, consisting of the chairman of the board of directors and twenty-six members elected by the board and twenty-seven members elected by ballot by the copartners in proportion to the numbers in each station. The three trustees under the scheme are one director, one officer, and one copartner workman, in whose names the investments are made annually in the company's stock. One of the two auditors, whose duty it is to compare the copartners' pass-books with the general account, is elected by the employees. The committee meets about once a quarter. In addition to its formal business the committee acts as a channel of communication between the management and the men. Grievances are ventilated and suggestions are made for improvement in the sanitary and other conditions of work, though general discussion on such topics as wages and the cost of living would probably be ruled out of order. It was the Co-partnership Committee which in 1897 settled and presented to the workers for acceptation the rules of the accident fund, a notable feature in which is the jury system dating back to 1892. Juries of twelve workmen investigate the causes of each accident and return a verdict, not hesitating to say whether any blame attaches to any official or workman, or whether the plant, machinery, or means of protection were defective (Rules xxii., 6). Furthermore, the Copartnership Committee watches certain cases belonging to the superannuation fund, and its most recent task has been provided by the National Insurance Act. The rules for the approved society which has been formed among the company's employees have been drawn up by the Copartnership Committee, assisted by additional representatives of the employees co-opted for the purpose. Similar work is doubtless done in other firms by organisation which is not styled Copartnership, but it is necessary to mention its existence because the success of Copartnership on its distinctive financial side has been assisted by the democratic machinery which works in it and about it.

The Copartnership Committee is the natural accompaniment of the bonus scheme, and is to be found in most, if not all, of the gas companies practising Copartnership. But there is one further feature peculiar to the South Metropolitan and South Suburban Companies, namely, the representation of the workers on the board of directors. The former company has had two workmen directors since 1898, and one clerk director since 1901 ; the

latter, two workmen directors since 1905. The
present employee-directors in the South Metropolitan
are a foreman of the gasfitters, an ordinary coke-
filler, and a chief clerk in a branch works. The
workmen and office staff vote separately, so that
the elections are genuinely representative of each
class. " The experiment," said Sir George Livesey
in 1908, " has given unalloyed satisfaction to
directors, officials, and workmen."[1] Now no one
requires to be convinced of the theoretical advantages
to both masters and men of having the workers'
point of view fairly and freely represented on the
board of management. The need for it grows each
day as the unit of production becomes bigger, and
the more personal relation of earlier days gives
way to the soullessness of the joint-stock company.
What is wanted is proof of its practicability, and
this the South Metropolitan and South Suburban
Companies, under the influence of a strong personality, have given to the world.

We have already observed that the interest of
consumers is formally safeguarded by the provision
that an increase of bonus is contingent upon a
reduction in the price of gas. When the company
serves a working-class district, a further incidental
advantage arises from Copartnership. About a
third of the South Metropolitan's trade is with the

[1] Livesey, " Copartnership," p. 11.

working classes. Its workmen, who largely live
in the area thus supplied, are a link between the
company and its consumers. They understand
the wants of working-class families, hear their
complaints and suggestions, and communicate these
to the management. In return they recommend
to their neighbours new or improved uses of gas.
Such zeal is perhaps carried to excess when, as we
are told [1] of one Copartnership company, the men
threatened to boycott the tobacco shop of a certain
town councillor who was rash enough to propose
the substitution of electricity for gas in the public
lighting.

The growth of municipal enterprise raises the
question as to whether it is desirable or possible
to introduce Copartnership among municipal
employees. Recent experience has shown that
municipalities as well as companies may have to
face labour trouble in the acute form of strikes.
It is doubtless desirable that the municipality should
lead the way in model conditions of employment ;
but if its employees by the direct pressure of a strike
or the indirect pressure of their votes thereby extort
wages very considerably higher than those prevailing
in the district for a similar class of work, there is no
clear gain to the public or even to the working class
as a whole. For either the rates or the price of the

[1] Livesey, " Copartnership," p. 29.

municipal services will be raised, and some of the burden will be borne by other working-men. But though municipal Copartnership may be desirable, it is less easy of application. For the municipality can fall back upon the ratepayer ; and a scheme of Copartnership based on municipal profit or municipal charges might degenerate into a form of indirect taxation, while further difficulties would arise over the investment of bonus in municipal stock. The one municipality which is sometimes said to practise profit-sharing, namely, the town of Stafford, in its gas and electricity departments, has, in fact, a scheme of gain-sharing only. For the bonus, which is all paid out in cash, does not vary with the profits of the departments, but with the amount by which the labour cost of manufacturing and distributing gas falls below a figure decided by the corporation to be reasonable.

The lesson of those successful experiments in the gas industry is, in part, the lesson which lies hid in the revolutionary Syndicalism of modern France. Both are a protest against the unsatisfactory status of the wage-earner under capitalism. Both aim at restoring that closeness of feeling between the worker and his work out of which enthusiasm and passion are born. The syndicalist dreams of an industrial society controlled by the workers of each trade, and believes that his zeal to smash the existing *régime* will certify his ability to dispense with the stupidity of the employer and the tyranny of the State in the *régime* which is to follow. The copartner is more modest, he believes that labour has need of capital even as capital of labour, and that mental and manual effort are equally entitled to their remuneration. The early economists, it is true, thought too much of production and too little of distribution. But the present age is inclining to the opposite error of forgetting that in the long run a high rate of dividend per head can only be obtained by a high annual output. Just as there are wastes of competition, so also there is waste in the long drawn battles of collective bargaining. Strikes should never indeed be judged by the immediate loss of wage or output; but if some strikes, by strengthening the respect of one party for the other, discourage future aggression, other strikes deepen mutual suspicion and lead to the expenditure of time and effort in concerting or defeating (as the case may be) persistent appeals to force. It is a dull mechanic ideal which can only conceive of progress by wedge and screw. After all, masters or men, we are citizens of the same country. Is freedom so jealous a handmaid that she cannot suffer experiments which demand mutual trust ? If so, then indeed is freedom barren and the outlook for Democracy black. If Copartnership is to be rejected because it does not assure prosperity in addition to sharing it when it accrues, then Democracy had better drop its claim to freedom and write itself " Slave—to be ridden by the expert."

CHAPTER IV

THE material on which the following analysis is based is derived in about equal proportions from England and France. In addition to the English schemes which we have already examined in detail, the recent Board of Trade Report [1] adduces about one hundred more. The French schemes summarised in M. Albert Trombert's "Practical Guide to Profit-Sharing," [2] also amount to more than one hundred, and the same writer notices a number of others in the United States of America, Germany, and elsewhere. Following the requirements recommended by previous international congresses on Profit-sharing (Paris 1889, 1896, 1900), the English Report admits only those schemes "in which an employer agrees with his employees that they shall receive in partial remuneration of their labour and in addition to their wages a share fixed beforehand in the profits realised by the undertaking to which the profit-

[1] Report on Profit-Sharing and Labour Copartnership in the United Kingdom [Cd. 6496] 1912.

[2] A. Trombert, "La Participation aux bénéfices." Paris, 1912. Librairie Chaix, Rue Bergere 20—the official publishers of the "Société pour l'étude de la participation."

sharing scheme relates." The payment of bonus on output, premiums proportionate to savings effected in production, commission on sales, and other systems under which the amount of the bonus depends upon the quality or amount of the output or volume of business, irrespective of the rate of profit earned, are not reckoned as profit-sharing. M. Trombert's conditions seem to be in one respect less exacting, for he includes about twenty French schemes "*sans quantum déterminé*" and vouches for them in the following terms—" While they share profits without previously divulging the rate, nevertheless they have formulated in a precise and generally complete manner rules which govern their policy."[1] These are the marginal cases in France, just as several schemes of privileged deposits are on the border-line in England. But on the whole the understanding of the term profit-sharing is the same in both of our sources.

A statement of the percentage figure of profit shared is of little value apart from inside knowledge of each case. For its significance will be different, according as the firm is small or large, according as it has a high wages bill of skilled workers or an unusually heavy proportion of capital expenditure, according as it is in form a public company in which the costs of management are included in the expenses

[1] A. Trombert, *op. cit.*, p. 28.

of production, or a private company in which the
profit is the owner's only remuneration. The
declaration of an initial fixed dividend to share
capital is now becoming a frequent device in English
copartnerships and it is a suggestive device, serving
to indicate that capital first takes a moderate wage
and then shares surplus profit with labour. But
we must repeat the warning that the guarantee
of moderation is only formal. There are forms of
capitalisation in which a 5 per cent. dividend on
ordinary share capital is more than moderate.

Both in England and France the distribution of
profit to labour is most commonly made in proportion
to the amount earned by each worker in the period
to which the distribution relates. The variations
on this simple form are not more than modifications
of it. Sometimes, mainly in France, a service
ranging from five years to one is required before
participation begins. Sometimes, again mainly in
France, the individual quantum is determined by
seniority, or by seniority plus wages, or by wages
augmented progressively for the higher paid workers.
It may be mentioned that in Denmark in virtue of
the law of March 15, 1903, the authority administer-
ing the State Railways allots to the workers a bonus
which varies with the dividend earned on the capital.
For this purpose the workers are divided into a
number of grades. Different quotas are assigned to

the different grades, but the quota of each grade is distributed equally among the persons composing it.[1]

In about three-fifths of the English schemes the bonus is paid in cash without further condition. A good case is that of Messrs Clarke, Nickolls & Coombs, Ltd.,[2] a London firm of confectionery makers which, since 1890, has paid out a total of £172,025 in cash bonus. £13,250, the amount paid in 1911, was equal to 2s. 10d. per £ on the wages of the 2000 employees participating, this being in accordance with the agreement by which the employees are given one-half of the surplus profits of the firm after the payment of 6 per cent. on its capital. Though the workers are encouraged to purchase shares in the business, and though, in fact, their holding is now considerable, yet perfect freedom attaches to the acceptance and use of the bonus. "You may belong to a union or not, as you like, you receive your share of the bonus in cash and may save or squander it just as you please. The bonus is given not from philanthropic, but from purely business motives, and it must be earned before it can be paid. Some friends of profit-sharing object to our system of paying the bonus in cash, but after twenty years' experience, I still believe that for our business it is the right system." (Extract from the speech by the head of the firm at the twentieth

[1] Trombert, *op. cit.*, pp. 11, 59.   [2] Board of Trade Report, 1912, pp. 36-8.

H

distribution, 1910.)   Now the Labour Copartnership Association, in its twenty-sixth report for 1911
(p. 14), very reasonably stigmatises as a defect of
many profit-sharing schemes the fact that " there
is little effort made to pass from simple profit-
sharing to capital-owning, though all experience
seems to show that the effect of the latter is far
and away more beneficial." But as this firm itself
argues, regard must be paid to the nature of the
business. It happens to be one which is situated
in London, and employs a large proportion of young
girls, some of them only temporarily. The advantages of a formal scheme of. share-holding by
employees are at their minimum, where many of
the workers are young persons who will probably
leave at an early age on marriage. It would be
imprudent to force such people into the technicalities
and risks of share-holding, and probably disastrous
to meet these objections by extending to young
girls or their nominees voting power and a share
in the control. The only practicable alternative
is the devotion of the bonus to a provident fund,
and this is actually done in the case of employees
with less than fifteen months' service. If extended
beyond this limit it might suffer from the objection
that the savings of the girl are best grouped with
those of her family in the manifold savings institutions
which London provides.

The profit-sharing and pension arrangements of Sir W. P. Härtley, jam manufacturer of Aintree, Lancs., should be studied in the same light. Details of these arrangements, which have now worked smoothly for many years, are not included in the Board of Trade's Report, inasmuch as the firm is a private one and does not publish a formal scheme. In 1912, on the twentieth anniversary of profit-sharing, £4650 was distributed, bringing the total from the origin up to £71,155.

Messrs Spillers & Bakers, Ltd., millers and biscuit manufacturers of Cardiff, began profit-sharing in 1900. After paying 6 per cent. on capital they divide the surplus *pro rata* on capital and wages. In addition they accept deposits from employees, which carry a fixed minimum of interest, plus half the difference between this and the total dividend paid on share capital, with a maximum limit of 7 per cent. In 1911, 708 out of 1350 employees participated in bonus and 356 had deposits averaging £34 per head. The firm writes [1]: "Although the recent critical labour conditions have some-what severely tested harmonious relations between employer and employed, we are inclined to think that had we not had this profit-sharing arrangement, matters would have been worse with us ; it certainly cannot be pronounced a ' cure,' but it might possibly

[1] Board of Trade Report, 1912, p. 72.

become such if it had not so strongly aroused the resentment of the more advanced labour leaders." We may place by the side of this the opinion of the Prudential Assurance Co., Ltd., which has paid cash bonuses out of surplus profit since 1907, 17,963 employees out of 20,664 being eligible in 1911. " The profit-sharing scheme has proved eminently satisfactory, and has been greatly appreciated by the staff. The Company has never been troubled with strikes. . . . The annual distribution of a share of the profits undoubtedly enables the Company to show its appreciation of the untiring efforts of a hard-working staff which they are anxious to suitably reward."

There is a difference between the processes of making biscuits and assuring lives ; and there is a very great difference between the two businesses with regard to the atmosphere which surrounds them and the relation of the personnel to the Labour Movement. Insurance clerks do not strike and rarely form trade unions, whether their masters be generous or mean, and whether, where generous, they share profits or pay unusually high wages. A manufacturer employing manual labour in a district of advanced unionism has altogether special difficulties to contend with. Anyone who has lectured in such a district knows that the bulk of opinion is against profit-sharing and Copartnership.

Probably not a few employers could confirm the experience alluded to by Sir W. G. Watson, chairman of the Maypole Dairy Co., in his address to the shareholders, February 1913 : " A few months ago he prepared for general adoption a scheme of Copartnership, but he regretted it was hardly acceptable to the representatives of Trade Unions who saw it, because he had suggested therein that only a proportion of all increases in profit made (after the adoption of profit-sharing and Copartnership) should go to the employees (in addition to their wages). He was told the trade union view was that all increases should go to employees. Unfortunately, he found it difficult to induce employers, who took all the risks of loss, to give the whole of all increases in profits to their employees." But are the workers or their Trade Unions always to blame ? If all that employers propose to distribute is the surplus, or a part of the surplus, above the average of the total profits of the previous three or five years, and if they recommend copartnership to their fellow employers on the ground that it involves them neither in risk nor in loss, can they expect it to meet with a very enthusiastic reception from working men ?

Nevertheless, insurance companies and other businesses where unionism is not militant are wise to be forward with experiments in social harmony.

In France, profit-sharing has long been common among insurance companies and savings institutions (*caisses d'épargne*). In the former—M. Trombert gives a list of twelve—the organisation is sometimes very elaborate. The *Union*, a fire insurance company, and the *Compagnie d'Assurances Générales* began profit-sharing in 1838 and 1850 respectively, and the principle of both is the same.[1] The distribution is made according to salary, but instead of being paid out in cash it is credited to individual account and accumulated as capital with interest at 4 per cent. The capital sum can only be enjoyed after a long period of service, twenty-five to thirty years, or on the attainment of an age limit of sixty to sixty-five ; and the enjoyment must take the form of the yield from investment in a life annuity, French *Rentes*, or railway debentures.

The rules of the *Compagnie d'Assurances Générales* stipulate that an *employé* [2] leaving before twenty-five years' service, whether on his own or the company's notice, forfeits all claim on the fund in which his account stands. The clause of forfeiture has given rise to very considerable discussion, especially in view of a law of 1890 which throws doubt on its legality.

[1] Trombert, pp. 214-231.

[2] " Employé " is hard to translate. In France, it means a member of the office staff, a salaried official, a shop hand. The English " employee " and American " employé " include both " employés " and " ouvriers."

Some of the companies have argued that it is a necessary method of self-defence, and that their servants would be drawn away by the offer of higher pay from rival companies if they were able to take with them the proceeds of the liberality of their old employers. The spokesmen of the *employés* have retorted that forfeiture means slavery and associates savings with the company when they should rather be the patrimony of a worker's family. The Congress of 1901 sympathised with this view by passing a resolution that " save in exceptional circumstances, of which master and companies must be the judges on their own responsibility, it is advisable not to introduce forfeiture clauses into contracts of profit-sharing." The present position is as follows. The old tontine element, whereby sums standing to the credit of workers prematurely deceased reverted to the general fund, has been uniformly abandoned. In the *Union* the forfeiture clause has disappeared : " the credits are now all of them the object of an acquired right." In the *Compagnie d'Assurances Générales* it remains, but in practice is leniently interpreted : " the management reserves the power of taking account of the gravity of offences committed by an *employé* who is discharged and of remitting to him a portion of his fund." It should be borne in mind that insurance is not a business which meets short seasons by a reduction of staff nor one in which transference from firm to firm is a normal feature of advancement. However, there can be little doubt that any parallel development in England ought to be associated with full ownership of the reserved savings after the model set by the South Metropolitan Gas Company.

The devotion of all or most of the bonus to a provident fund is as rare in England as it is common in France. Messrs Cassell & Co., Ltd., printers and publishers, is the only big concern which shares profits on this principle. In France the schemes of the insurance companies are paralleled by others of the same order in various departments of commercial and industrial enterprise. The firms' hold on the credits ranges from the explicit clause of forfeiture to absolute freedom of disposition. A middle way is common. The firm distinguishes dismissal without blame from dismissal for offence or departure into rival service. In the former case the worker forfeits nothing, in the latter he is treated at the firm's discretion. Where, as sometimes happens, the firms place the sums standing to the individual account of workers with an institution outside their own establishment, such as the National Pension Fund, they necessarily part with the power of forfeiture. One such firm, the *Imprimerie Chaix*, which specialises in the printing of railway matter, had from 1872 to 1895 a scheme of part payment in cash and part payment in Government securities. In 1895 this was replaced to the satisfaction of the 614 participants by the allocation of the whole sum to the National Pension Fund.

We have perhaps over-emphasised the question of forfeiture. M. Alfred Courcy, the director of the *Compagnie d'Assurances Générales*, who supported its retention, and M. Charles Robert, who was converted to its abolition, were at one in striving for two more fundamental objects, which the International Congress of 1889 heartily endorsed. One was to make profit-sharing a circumstance of permanent worth to the recipient, the other was to associate the recipient's family in the eventual enjoyment of the benefits. A cash bonus, urge the organisers of profit-sharing in France, is in the worker's eyes a gratuity to which when spent he does not give a further thought and not, as it should be, a seed from which good fruit will spring. On the other hand, the old-fashioned provision of a life annuity just misses the thing that is dearest to the French heart, the making of a patrimony. These same two desideratives have been reiterated time and again by English profit-sharers, and it was because it gave permanence to the fruits of united effort not less than because it gave to all an active interest in the Company's prosperity that Sir George

Livesey recommended to others his own scheme of Copartnership.

The devotion of the bonus to permanent purposes offers a further very great advantage. Masters or boards of management may be anxious to take counsel with their own men, but unable to find a suitable medium. Workers' delegations are apt to be formal things, and in very few businesses can representatives of the men be added forthwith to the managing body. For at all costs the master must remain master in his relations with individual men. But the finance and management of provident funds can be separated from the finance and management of the business. Here is an excellent channel of communication between masters and men, one in which real scope can be found for representative democracy and joint executive work. In France, the insurance companies have in general reserved to themselves the control of their provident funds, but many other firms, as M. Trombert says,[1] "have instituted consultative committees, whose members chosen from the ranks of the personnel advise with the head of the house on possible ways of improving the provident institutions. Real family councils, these committees do excellent work. Far from arousing distrust they make for conciliation and union. They frequently discharge with attentive

[1] *Op. cit.*, p. 150.

care and unremitting zeal the functions entrusted
to them by their employer or fellow-workers."
The writer notes the existence of some twenty such
consultative committees in France. Their work
clearly resembles that done by the Copartnership
committees in the English gas companies. English
employers, who, from the nature of their businesses,
cannot conveniently or prudently associate their
workers in share-holding, are in this respect at a
disadvantage in comparison with their brothers in
France. They may want to do more than divide
profits, but share-holding being by supposition impracticable, and a provident fund pure and simple
being uncongenial to English notions of liberty, they
have to forego the intercourse that the consultative
committee so happily provides. The committee
affords to the workers a twofold advantage. It
educates them in self-government; and, what in
England is a more pressing want (for the workmen
of England through their friendly societies, trade
unions, and co-operative stores have given to themselves their own self-government), it brings them
into relations with the firm that are at once human
and equal. A session at a common table has often
been the solvent of industrial disputes, and the
advocates of Copartnership seek to make of it a
permanent instrument of executive harmony.

We have seen in the previous chapter the characteristic turn which Copartnership has recently taken in England. The generalisation of company structure and the elasticity of trusteeship both favour share-holding by employees. We have examined the two great experiments at the top of the scale. At the bottom of it we may place the schemes of privileged deposits. Sometime before 1878—the precise date is not known—Sir Joseph Whitworth the distinguished Manchester engineer, " told his own workmen that if they liked to invest part of their wages in the firm he would be their savings bank, and would give them the same dividend that he got himself on his own capital."[1] In 1896 his business was amalgamated with that of Sir W. G. Armstrong and others, and the scheme of profit-sharing deposits was extended in a slightly modified form to the whole of the employees of the amalgamated company. Deposits of not less than 1s. and not more than £1 of the depositor's weekly wages are received from persons in the company's employ each week, and used in the business. The deposits carry a fixed interest of 4 per cent., and, in addition, a bonus equal to half the difference between this fixed rate and the dividend payable on the shares of the company, but so that interest and bonus together shall not in any case exceed 10 per cent. Deposits are

[1] *Cf.* Board of Trade Report, 1894 [C. 7458], p. 49.

withdrawable on short notice, and, of course, not liable to forfeiture. In December 1911, 2788 employees held on deposit a total of £241,432. In addition, some employees have made private investments in the ordinary securities of the company. The number of persons employed at the works in 1911 varied from 15,812 to 15,953.[1]

With this we may compare the scheme still operating in the United States Steel Corporation, and the scheme instituted in 1909 and abandoned a year later at the shipbuilding yards of Furness, Withy & Co. The tenth report of the United States Steel Corporation of December 1911 states that " in continuation of the plan observed in previous years, beginning with 1903, the employés of the United States Steel Corporation and the subsidiary companies were, in January 1912, offered the privilege of subscribing for Preferred or Common Stock. Subscriptions were received from 36,946 employés for an aggregate of 30,169 shares of Preferred and 30,735 of Common Stock. The subscription price was fixed at $110·00 per share for the Preferred and $65·00 per share for the Common Stock. The allowances for special compensation or bonus to be paid subscribers who retain their stock were fixed at $5·00 per share per year for the Preferred and $3·50 per share

[1] Board of Trade Report, 1912, pp. 41-2.

annually for the Common Stock." The employés are allowed to pay by monthly instalments over three years, and the maximum which may be subscribed varies from 5 per cent. of the annual salary of the highest paid employees to 20 per cent. of the salary of the lowest paid. The shares of this combine are the object of international gambling on a large scale, and in December 1911 a new cause of uncertainty was introduced by the proceedings against the Corporation under the Anti-Trust Act. The Common Stock then fell to 52 from a maximum of 83 earlier in the year, rose to 70 in January 1912, fell back to under 60 after the big fire in New York, rose again to 70 in midsummer, and then collapsed, along with many speculative stocks on the outbreak of the Balkan War. During all this period the Corporation was reporting bright prospects in trade and growing quantities of unfilled orders. The holder of Steel Common, whether a worker or private investor, finds himself inevitably in an atmosphere of speculation. A prudent worker, therefore, as we in England judge prudence, would invest in the Preferred Stock. Even this fluctuates disconcertingly in capital value : in 1909 the 7 per cent. Preference stood at 130 and in January 1913 at 110. It is true that the interest itself is a fixed and fairly assured return, but this prevents even a formal correlation between the efforts of workers and their share in the Corporation's profits from year to year. Messrs Armstrong's deposit scheme may not excite the workers by high dividends and the prospects of appreciation in capital value, but at least it gives a sober and intelligent expression to the notion of a joint interest in a common concern.

The scheme published by the late Lord Furness in October 1908 was more ambitious. It followed on a protracted strike in the ship-building industry in the north of England and was intended to combine profit-sharing with machinery for the preservation of industrial peace. In a conference at West Hartlepool, October 7th, 1908, Sir Christopher Furness, chairman of Furness, Withy & Co., invited the employees in the ship-building yards to become limited copartners in the ship-building, as distinct from the ship-owning, department of the company's business. The shares of employees were to be paid in instalments by 5 per cent. deductions from wages. They were guaranteed interest at 4 per cent., and after the ordinary capital had received 5 per cent. they were to receive a further dividend at the same rate per cent. as the further dividend on the ordinary shares. A Works Council, containing representatives of the company and employees, was to manage the scheme and to consider in addition all matters likely to lead to industrial

disputes. If the Works Council failed to settle
any difference it was to be referred to a court of
arbitration, but "under no consideration shall
employees strike against the directions and decision
of their copartners governing the administration
of the business."[1] On the advice of the Trade
Union leaders the scheme was given a trial. For
the year 1909 those workers who took up shares
got a dividend of 9 per cent., but at the end of
the year the employees by a small majority voted
against the continuation of the scheme. We have
no inside knowledge of the events, but it certainly
looks as though in this case the management was
"giving too little and asking too much." The
men were requested to surrender the weapon of a
strike, a weapon which is sometimes very effective
in a highly organised industry like ship-building.
The company's case would have been stronger if
they had paid out of profits the sums, or at any
rate a part of the sums, destined for the acquisition
of shares. The British workman is very jealous
of any interference with the free disposal of his
standard wage. Successful profit sharers from
Godin to Sir George Livesey have always laboured
to make the distinction between wage and bonus
absolute.

Messrs Hazell, Watson & Viney, Ltd., printers

[1] See report in *Times*, Oct. 8, 1908.

and bookbinders of London and Aylesbury, have
for the last eighteen years encouraged their workers
to become shareholders in the company by offering
on preferential terms shares payable by weekly
instalments of 1s. per share. In every case the
shares have been sold at about three-quarters of
their market value, so that each share sold represents
a bonus of £4 to £5 to the purchaser. An insurance
scheme is combined with the purchase, which provides
that in the event of the employee's death before
the instalments are completed the share becomes
the property of his heirs without further payment.
The number of £10 shares now held by employees
is 1219. They entitle the holders to the ordinary
voting rights and the proportion borne by the
votes of these employees to the total of all votes that
could be given at a general meeting is approximately
4·9 per cent. When an employee wishes to realise
his capital or leaves the business for any cause
except old age, he must sell his shares to another
employee at the same reduced price. In this way,
shares intended to benefit employees remain in
the hands of those actually working for the firm.

Now, outwardly, Mr Hazell's scheme is akin to
that of the United States Steel Corporation, but
the atmosphere is remarkably different. For here
share-holding is but one item in a many-sided
endeavour to enrich the lot of the 1400 employees

I

in the firm. In a foreword to the little book which describes these endeavours, Mr Hazell writes :— "All that is set down here has been a gradual growth, beginning, in some cases, on a minute scale, more than thirty years ago, and has been developed and adapted to the changing conditions as the years went on. . . . I gratefully acknowledge the co-operation I have always received from my co-workers in the business, some of whom have passed away ; without their aid many of the schemes herein set forth would have died of inanition." The list, which is of noble length, amounts in sum to the following :—

Shares held by employees (at market value) . . .	£18,000
Savings Bank Deposits . . .	13,324
Provident Fund	14,544
Staff Pension Fund . . .	1,604
Thrift Fund (for house purchase, etc.), total loans granted, £13,472, amount repaid . . .	9,327
	£56,799

To this must be added sick funds, recreation clubs, institutes, allotments, shows—more than a score of things in all. The presence of these supplementary activities vouches for the right spirit of the financial arrangements, and in Copartnership the spirit is always more important than the letter.

We come, in conclusion, to two novel schemes, which are still in the stage of experiment.

Messrs Foster, Son & Co.,[1] builders, of Padiham, Lancs., have established within the firm an employees' investment society, registered in April 1903 under the Industrial and Provident Society's Act as "Foster's Employees, Ltd." After 5 per cent. has been paid on capital the surplus profit is appropriated as follows :—One-half goes to the managers and shareholders as a further remuneration, and one-half to the employees' society to be applied to the purchase of shares in the company for the benefit of individual employees. The bonus paid by the company in respect of an employee who belongs to the society is accumulated until it suffices to purchase a fully paid share, which share is held not in the company but in the employees' investment society itself. The bonus paid in respect of employees who are not members of the society is credited collectively to a Non-members' Provident Fund. The investment society deals in the company's capital and draws dividend like a private shareholder. The dividends thus accruing to the society are utilised for the advantage of its members. At present

[1] Board of Trade Report, 1912, pp. 49-52.

the members draw 5 per cent. on their shares, and not until a reserve fund equal to 25 per cent. of the value of the society's holdings has been formed can they draw an additional dividend. Of the total capital of the company, namely, 4000 shares of £1 each, 764 are owned by the investment society. This entitles the society to one-fourth of all the votes that can be given at a general meeting of shareholders, and out of the four directors of the company two are employees appointed by the investment society.

By the Limited Partnerships Act of 1907 it is now possible for the employees of a private firm to acquire a collective interest in the business with strictly limited financial liability and no power of interference in the management. But, as the Act says, "a limited partner may by himself or his agent at any time inspect the books of the firm and examine into the state and prospects of the partnership business and may advise with the partners thereon." Messrs Gilbert,[1] boot manufacturers of Nantwich, Cheshire, have used the Act for the purpose of representing their workers in the body of the firm. The employees' society is registered as Gilbert Bros. Employees, Ltd., and is related to the general partners in much the same way as in the Maison Leclaire the Mutual Aid Society is related to the managing partners. Each

[1] Board of Trade Report, 1912, pp. 46-9.

member of the society is credited with the amount received by the society as dividend on his wages or salary. Interest is paid on this sum at the rate of 5 per cent., when the society's profits suffice thereto, and surplus profit is devoted to reserve. Messrs Gilbert, the general partners, furthermore bind themselves after drawing their salaries and 5 per cent. interest on their capital to devote the remainder in the manner described, *i.e.* to the investment society for the account of its individual members. As the amount of capital belonging to the employees increases, that belonging to the general partners is to be decreased, until the latter are paid out and the society becomes virtually a workers' productive society. In 1909 sixty-six of the ninety-two persons employed in the firm were members of Gilbert Bros. Employees, Ltd.

CHAPTER V

RUMOUR has it that a certain profit-sharer died and went to his place of rest in the Elysian fields, to whose proprietor he forthwith proposed a scheme of profit-sharing. So the first year they grew wheat, and the profit-sharer took the tops leaving his partner the straw. Next year they grew turnips, and the profit-sharer, for fairness' sake, gave his partner the tops, taking the turnips for himself. The moral of which is that Copartnership, to be acceptable, must be fair and square. But what is fairness ? Fairness consists in a right appreciation of the thing that is to be shared, namely, surplus profit or prosperity. "But," the critic will object, as the critics have objected for the last fifty years, "if Labour shares in profits, ought it not in fairness to share in losses ? " This was said to Godin. Let us mark Godin's answer. "This argument is specious. It is not true in effect that Labour is not exposed to chances of loss : its losses are felt in a form different from those of Capital, but they are none the less real for that. Is it not a loss for Labour when the course of industry necessitates

134

a reduction of wage ? Is it not a loss for Labour when unemployment arrives and wages cease with the closing of the workshops ? " [1] Godin was right. We do not insure employers against unemployment, and we may not ask employees to imperil their standard wage.

The labour crisis in the spring of 1912 elicited many suggestions for the future avoidance of industrial disputes. One of these was a Bill intended to further the adoption of Copartnership, " The Companies Amendment Act (Copartnership) Bill," [238]. The explanatory memorandum states that " it is provided that the standard rate of wages shall be taken to correspond with a standard return of 5 per cent. on all paid-up capital, and when the return is higher than 5 per cent. the employer becomes entitled to a bonus calculated at one-twentieth of his existing wages for every extra 1 per cent. paid in dividend. . . . Further, in order to meet the varying circumstances of different industries, it is provided that in the case of registered companies the Board of Trade may allow other regulations to be substituted in individual instances, and in particular may allow a lower rate of bonus when salaries and wages bear a specially high proportion of the annual cost of the business of the Company." Legislation can do many things, and the Board of Trade can do

[1] "Mutualité Sociale," p. 56.

some things, but neither can profitably interfere
in the promotion of Copartnership.   At any rate,
if employers want a measure of this sort—and
almost certainly they do not—let them first place
on the Statute book a legal minimum wage in every
industry in which it is proposed to introduce compulsory Copartnership.

The French have not been quick to resist the
intrusion of the State into the domain of economic
organisation.   The workers' co-operative productive
societies in Paris enjoy material privileges in tender-
ing for municipal contracts, and co-operative rural
credit is richly dowered by the Bank of France.
Where the State can intervene with advantage,
France may be trusted to make the experiment.
All the more remarkable, therefore, is the decision
come to by the Bordeaux Congress in November
1912.   " The greatest peril which profit-sharing
could encounter, the greatest obstacle in the way
of its development, would be a law which makes
profit-sharing obligatory.   We can only admit
profit-sharing as a voluntary measure." This was
the unanimous vote of a French Congress.   When,
therefore, we say to the English politicians, " hands
off ! " we are by no means guilty of unsympathy
or anachronism.   For freedom is the breath of life
to Copartnership ; if compelled by law, Copartnership would lose all its stimulus, and become, in fact,

a tax on industrial production. Laws are needed to endow citizenship by way of insurance against sickness, old age, and unemployment, and to-day in England the endowment is not niggardly. But the funds from which the endowments come are produced ultimately by private enterprise, and while this remains so, it is to the common interest that the heads of business organisations should be allowed free scope in the allocation of wages above the minimum of subsistence and, above all, free scope in the yet further allocation of something that is additional to the wage itself. " *Autant de maisons pratiquant la participation, autant de règles distinctes, peut-on dire.*" [1]

Even at the end of our inquiry we are unable to state categorically the things which constitute Copartnership. For it is not so much a body of things as a body with a spirit in it. The movement towards share-holding by employees deserves from Englishmen the greater attention, because it is the line which English development is naturally taking. But there are some businesses which could not face the indefinite extension of capital holding which a huge and expanding concern like the South Metropolitan Gas Company, with its more or less closed market, can contemplate with equanimity. And there are other businesses which being themselves

[1] Article in *Le Temps*, Feb. 3, 1913.

young or composed mainly of juvenile workers could not profitably model themselves on the achievements of Port Sunlight. Each experiment must be adapted to the particular needs. Frenchmen will view the problem through French spectacles and examine with care the provident funds which are so often in their country the stepping-stone to further things. But on one point the students of both countries will find themselves in agreement. When they are studying successes they are studying personalities—studying, in fine, the stuff of which industrial chivalry is made.

APPENDIX I

HAVING been privileged to submit my account of Godin to Madame Prudhommeaux-Dallet, who spent all her youth at the Familistère, I take the liberty of reproducing in summary her very effective answer to my one criticism on Godin's works (*v.* page 44).

"The question must be considered historically, with reference to the conditions obtaining at the foundation of the Familistère and the state of mind of the people at that time. The personnel of the foundry were for the most part sceptical of, or indifferent to, the ideal which Godin set before them as a body. The workers who came to live with him, placing themselves and their families under his direct influence, were those who believed in him and accepted the idea of preparing themselves for the coming Association. Hence the privileges accorded to the residents in the Familistère. The workers being less numerous than now, entry into the Familistère was in fact possible, during the whole of Godin's life, to those of them who, moved thereto by strictly personal interest, decided to give up their separate apartments or little cottages, in order to 'pass from Class III to Class II and so to Class I.' It was, in fact, this interested motive which induced the greater part of the requests for admission from the time the Association was founded.

" One may say of the first generation of families admitted
to the Familistère, that it was, thanks to Godin's influence,
lifted morally beyond the level of the families who
remained outside, and that it justified thereby the
measures taken in its favour.   Since then things have
altered.   First, the children of these families fitted for
association by their education in the schools, have in their
turn become residents and thus made vacancies rare.
Secondly, the demands for admission have increased by
reason of the pecuniary and other advantages attaching to
residence in the Palais Social; and, as a result of this, and
of the slackening of moral enthusiasm, there has been a
decline in the real worth of those who were intended to
form the *élite* of the place and were privileged accordingly.
Thirdly, the business, which used to flourish on the
working of patents and made good profits with a relatively
small staff, has changed in character and requires increasingly manual labour.   Hence, though the turnover
has thereby been considerably enlarged, profits have not
grown proportionately.

" Thus the number of Auxiliaries (Helpers) and Participants (Class III) grows without it being practically
possible to assure to a constantly increasing number of
families the advantages yielded by full association in the
Familistère.   For the workers in Class III are associated
in the enterprise as *individuals*; whereas membership in
Classes I and II places the whole *family* in the Association.
The latter status involves the Association, in the event of
industrial depression, or worse still, of war, in respon-
sibilities of so serious an order that Godin himself declared

that one could not, under the present *régime* of unregulated competition, increase the number of dwellings
in the Familistère, without compromising the very existence of the scheme. To insure 550 families, men, women,
children, and old persons against sickness, old age, and
indigence, and to equip them with education and instruc-
tion, already costs more than 80,000 francs (£3200) per
annum ; and this sum would have to be more than trebled
to assure these advantages to the families of all the
workers. It would involve an expense, which in ordinary
years would almost swallow up the divisible profits, in
addition to necessitating large new buildings, which would
tie up the Society's capital—with the result that the
scheme of keeping the ownership of the concern in the
hands of active workers, which is at present successfully
maintained, would be overthrown. In other words, an
industrial establishment cannot, by itself alone, reform
the world and realise perfect justice."

Madame Prudhommeaux-Dallet adds a further note
of equal value, with reference to p. 49.

" The Subsistence grant is not dependent on domi-
ciliary inspection, which would lend it the character of
charity, but issues of right, and is regulated on a pre-
determined scale. Let us suppose that A, a worker of
little skill, earning only a mediocre wage, has a child, and
that on the scale (the same for all) which is recognised as
necessary for the support of life, per member of the
family, his wages are insufficient to secure this minimum.
Then, without any request from the family, the Necessities
Fund pays him each fortnight the sum to which he is

entitled, until his situation changes, until, for example, an elder child earns wages, or until he himself passes on to better paid work.

"In order that the Committee, which administers this fund may keep in contact with each necessitous case, and in order that the sick visitors, male or female, may be able to control effectually the sick cases, it is necessary that the people should not be distributed at random among the different streets of the town, where supervision would be ineffective, if not inquisitorial. Only in this way can the assurance funds be kept clear of serious abuses."

BIBLIOGRAPHY

In English

Annual Reports of the Labour Copartnership Association, 6 Bloomsbury Square, London, W.C.

Board of Trade Reports :—
" Profit-Sharing," 1894 [C. 7458].

"Profit-Sharing and Labour Copartnership in the United Kingdom," 1912 [Cd. 6496].

" Industrial and Agricultural Co-operative Societies in the United Kingdom," 1912 [C. 6045].

C. Webb (ed. by). "Industrial Co-operation." Co-operative Union, Manchester, 1904.

Sedley Taylor. "Profit-Sharing between Capital and Labour." New York, 1886.

In French

The Society for the Study of Profit-sharing in France publishes its literature through the "Imprimerie Chaix," Rue Bergère 20, Paris, where the following may be obtained :—

"Congrès international de la participation aux bénéfices," Compte Rendu. Paris, 1900.

Albert Trombert. "La Participation aux bénéfices, guide pratique." Paris, 1912.

Dr Victor Böhmert, "La Participation aux bénéfices, en Allemagne, en Autriche, et en Suisse." Translated from German into French by A. Trombert. Paris, 1912.

"Bulletin de la Participation aux bénéfices" (three-monthly issue). The Society's official publication.

Charles Robert. "Leclaire, Biographie d'un homme utile." Paris, 1873.

D. F. Prudhommeaux.[1] "Familistère illustré, Résultats de vingt ans d'association," 1880-1900. Paris, 1900.

Ibid. "Les expériences sociales de" J.-B. A. Godin (1867-1878), Nimes, 1912.

[1] Translated into English and brought down to a later date by Aneurin Williams: "Twenty-eight years of Copartnership at Guise." Labour Co-partnership Association: London, 1908.

INDEX

K   145